BE SEATED

ALSO BY JAMES CROSS GIBLIN

The Truth About Unicorns

The Riddle of the Rosetta Stone
Key to Ancient Egypt

Let There Be Light
A Book About Windows

From Hand to Mouth
*Or, How We Invented Knives, Forks, Spoons,
and Chopsticks & the Table Manners
To Go With Them*

Milk
The Fight for Purity

The Truth About Santa Claus

Chimney Sweeps
Yesterday and Today

The Skyscraper Book

BE SEATED

A BOOK ABOUT CHAIRS

James Cross Giblin

ILLUSTRATED WITH PHOTOGRAPHS,
PRINTS, AND DRAWINGS

HarperCollins*Publishers*

FRONTISPIECE: Side chair made about 1902 by Frank Lloyd Wright for the Ward W. Willets house dining room. The Metropolitan Museum of Art, Purchase, Mr. and Mrs. David Lubart Gift, in memory of Katharine J. Lubart (1944–1975), 1978. (1978.189)

TITLE PAGE: Gerrit Rietveld's "Kinderstoel." Photo courtesy of Barry Friedman Ltd., New York.

Be Seated: *A Book About Chairs*
Copyright © 1993 by James Cross Giblin
All rights reserved. No part of this book may be used or reproduced in any manner whatsoever without written permission except in the case of brief quotations embodied in critical articles and reviews. Printed in the United States of America. For information address HarperCollins Children's Books, a division of HarperCollins Publishers, 10 East 53rd Street, New York, NY 10022.
Typography by Margaret M. Wagner
2   3   4   5   6   7   8   9   10
❖

Library of Congress Cataloging-in-Publication Data
Giblin, James.
    Be seated : a book about chairs / by James Cross Giblin.
        p.   cm.
    Includes bibliographical references (p.   ) and index.
    Summary: Chronicles the history, technological development, and social significance of chairs, in Europe, Africa, Asia, and the United States, from prehistory to the present.
    ISBN 0-06-021537-2. — ISBN 0-06-021538-0 (lib. bdg.)
    1. Chairs—Juvenile literature. [1. Chairs.] I. Title.
NK2715.G46   1993   92-25073
749'.32—dc20   CIP
                                                      AC

To the American art museums that have given me so much inspiration and pleasure —especially The Cleveland, The Metropolitan, The Museum of Modern Art, and the National Gallery.

❧

"I had three chairs in my house: one for solitude, two for friendship, three for society."

Henry David Thoreau,
in WALDEN

Acknowledgments

I am grateful to the following individuals and institutions for their help in providing information and illustrations: Sue Alexander; The Bettmann Archive; The Cleveland Museum of Art; The Cooper-Hewitt Museum of the Smithsonian Institution; The Dallas Museum of Art; Peter Danko & Associates; The Domino's Center for Architecture and Design; Michael Aase Fedele, Barry Friedman Ltd.; Horace Anguah-Dei, Assistant Information Officer, Embassy of Ghana, Washington; Håg, Inc.; Henry H. Hawley; The Historical Society of Pennsylvania; Jenai Taylor, The Knoll Group; The Metropolitan Museum of Art; Stephen G. Chappell, Herman Miller Inc.; Jim Murphy; Museum of Fine Arts, Boston; The Museum of Modern Art, New York; National Archives, Washington; National Gallery of Art, Washington; The New York Public Library; Barbara Mancuso, *New York Times* Pictures; The Philadelphia Museum of Art; Jeanne Prahl.

Special thanks to my editor, Barbara Fenton, who believed in the idea for this book from the time I first mentioned it.

—J.C.G.

Contents

Chapter One   Your Favorite Chair *1*

Chapter Two   Stools for Men and Chairs for Women *9*

Chapter Three   A Throne for the Master *25*

Chapter Four   Barbarian Couches *39*

Chapter Five   Who Gets to Sit in a Chair? *47*

Chapter Six   Chairs for Everyone *57*

Chapter Seven   From Simple to Overstuffed *71*

Chapter Eight   The Golden Stool of the Ashanti *87*

Chapter Nine   "A Machine for Sitting In" *99*

Chapter Ten   A Perfect Chair? *113*

Bibliography and Source Notes *123*

Index *131*

CHAPTER ONE

Your Favorite Chair

You probably have a favorite chair. It may be an easy chair with deep cushions, or a colonial-style rocking chair, or a modern chair with a canvas seat and a metal frame. In it, you like to read or watch television, talk on the phone, or maybe just sit back and snooze.

Whatever you do in the chair, you feel comfortable. That's why it's your favorite. And you probably assume that everyone else has his or her favorite chair, too.

If you do, you're mistaken. In many parts of the world, especially outside big cities, people don't sit on chairs at all. Instead they squat, kneel, or sit cross-legged on the floor or ground, and are comfortable doing so. Some health experts say these positions are better for the human body than sitting upright in a chair.

The Arab peoples of the Middle East are among those who customarily squatted on the ground. For centuries the Arabs were nomads who moved from place to place and lived in tents. They spent most of their lives at ground level, resting, eating, and sleeping on mats and rugs. Cushions and perhaps a wooden chest provided support for their backs.

The Arabs' lack of furniture made it easy for them to load their belongings onto pack animals when they traveled to the next campsite. Today many Arabs still follow the old ways, sitting and sleeping on rugs and pillows even though they now live in towns and cities.

A group of nomadic Arabs at rest. Nineteenth-century print from the Kubler Collection. Photo by Ken Pelka, The Cooper-Hewitt Museum of the Smithsonian Institution

The Japanese are another people who, until recently, usually knelt or squatted on the floors of their homes. Because earthquakes are frequent in Japan, the Japanese built lightweight, one-story houses of wood and furnished them with only a few chests and low tables. This made the houses less dangerous if a quake hit, because there was nothing heavy to fall on the occupants. It was also easier to rebuild the houses, and replace the furniture, if a quake damaged or destroyed them.

Chairs were unknown in traditional Japanese houses. Families knelt on the floor on rice-straw mats called *tatami*, and slept on them also. To help keep the mats clean, the Japanese removed their shoes before entering the house.

In those regions of the world where people sit in chairs, the practice appears to go back to prehistoric times. Perhaps people first got the idea from sitting on flat-topped rocks outside their cave homes. Later on, someone may have thought of carrying along flat pieces of stone or wood when the tribe moved from place to place. These could be laid on top of three or four rocks of approximately equal height to form stoollike seats.

Regular furniture making began in ancient Egypt and elsewhere more than five thousand years ago, when

Four Japanese girls kneel on a terrace to play a game while another strums a musical instrument. Hanging scroll by Hasegawa Yasumasa, painted about 1760. The Cleveland Museum of Art, The Kelvin Smith Collection, given by Mrs. Kelvin Smith, 85.258

people started to use tools to shape objects from wood. It was then that some clever craftsperson must have taken a flat piece of wood, bored three or four holes in the underside, and fitted wooden sticks into them. Thus the stool, the forerunner of the chair, was born.

Early stools were usually reserved for important people like kings and high priests. A ruler would sit on his stool, which was often placed on a low platform, and gaze down at his loyal subjects squatting on the ground below. Such royal stools were soon recognized as symbols of power and authority, and developed into the first thrones.

Not all ancient thrones were meant to be sat on. Some in India, where most people knelt or squatted on the ground, were simply rectangular platforms. The Buddha, founder of the Buddhist religion, was often shown on a platform throne. Sculptors usually portrayed him sitting with his legs crossed.

Most thrones did include seats, though. And from simple stools these seats gradually evolved into chairs with backs and arms. The back probably came first, and may originally have been an extension upward of the two rear legs, joined by a crosspiece. Arms were added later, and most likely began as extensions of the two front legs. These extensions were topped with flat armrests that were attached to the back of the throne on each side.

Over time, thrones in the ancient world became more and more elaborate. They were made from a great

A seated Buddha, sculpted in the Gandhara region of India in the first half of the third century A.D. The Cleveland Museum of Art, Leonard C. Hanna, Jr., Fund, 61.418

variety of materials—wood, stone, marble, even precious metals—and were finely carved and decorated.

Probably the most lavish of all ancient thrones was the one on which Solomon, King of the Hebrew people, sat in the ninth century B.C. The Old Testament describes it in the following words (1 Kings 10:18–20):

Moreover the king made a great throne of ivory, and overlaid it with the best gold.

The throne had six steps, and the back of the throne was round [curved] behind: and there were stays [arms] on either side of the seat, and two lions stood beside the stays.

And twelve lions stood there on the one side and on the other upon the six steps: there was not the like made in any kingdom.

The lions were probably carved out of stone, and perhaps they, like the throne, were covered with gold. We have no way of knowing, since no trace of King Solomon's throne remains today.

The basic pattern of Solomon's throne survives, however, in the chairs on which we sit. For every piece of seat furniture, whether an elaborate throne or a humble kitchen chair, has always had the same purpose: to support the weight of the human body. And there are only so many seat forms that can fulfill this purpose, since the ways in which people sit have changed little over the years.

While the essential form of the chair has stayed the same, there have been many variations in chair design through the centuries. This book singles out some of the most unusual and significant of these designs, many of which are still being manufactured. In fact, one of them may be your favorite chair.

The book also explores what the chairs reveal about those who first sat in them. For household furniture can provide some of the best and clearest insights into the daily lives of people . . . how they eat, rest, and sleep, and even how they relate to one another.

CHAPTER TWO

Stools for Men and Chairs for Women

When twentieth-century archaeologists excavated the tombs of Tutankhamen and other ancient Egyptian pharaohs, they discovered much more than mummies. Because the Egyptians believed in an afterlife, they furnished their rulers' tombs with all the things they would need in the hereafter.

The chambers were filled with beds and bedding, chests of clothing and jewelry, pottery vases and dishes, and seat furniture ranging from stools to thrones. Preserved in the dry, sealed tombs, most of the wooden chairs were as sturdy as the day they had been made over two thousand years before.

From these discoveries, and from Egyptian wall paintings, archaeologists could get a good picture of daily life in ancient Egypt.

The typical home of a prosperous city dweller in the XVIII dynasty (1570–1342 B.C.) was made of plastered and whitewashed mud brick, since lumber was scarce in the Nile Delta. An entrance hall led to the central living room, its roof supported by one or more columns. Off this room there would be several small bedrooms or storage rooms. The kitchen was located outdoors in a courtyard, so that smoke and heat from the cooking fire would not get into the house.

Such a house would not have contained much in the way of seat furniture. Only the very wealthy in ancient Egypt possessed a variety of chairs, while the poor usually squatted on mats made of reeds or palm fiber.

In a home like this one—occupied perhaps by a minor government official and his family—there would probably have been a dozen or so wooden stools, some with three legs and some with four. The stools were light enough for even small children to move from room to room as the need arose. There might also be a single wooden chair for the use of the head of the family. When the master wanted to change location, he or a servant carried the chair from the living room to the courtyard and back.

No one knows exactly when the Egyptians first began to make seat furniture. But examples of both stools

and chairs survive from the beginning of the Old Kingdom (about 3110 B.C.).

Egyptian stools came in many different styles, and
were used by all classes of people, up to and including
the Pharaoh. Egyptian workmen often sat on roughly
made three-legged stools, and these could be found in
humbler homes also. But there were much fancier
types: elaborately decorated stools with flared legs and
leather seats, and folding stools with legs that ended in
carved ducks' heads at the bottom.

The earliest Egyptian chairs had low backs but no
arms. Because good lumber was expensive as well as
scarce in Egypt, a chair would often be made of several
different kinds of wood. The seat might be of acacia or
sycamore from a local tree, while the back and legs
were of juniper or cedar imported from Syria.

In joining the pieces together, Egyptian woodwork-
ers used a new method of construction that they had
probably invented. This was the mortise and tenon, and
it is still employed by furniture makers today. First a
hole or groove, called a mortise, was cut into the side of
one piece of wood. Then a small projecting member,
called the tenon, was shaped from the end of another
piece. The woodworker inserted the tenon in the

The Egyptian sculptor Ipuy and his wife receive offerings to aid them in the afterlife. Note the wife's cat beneath her chair and the kitten playing on Ipuy's lap. Copy of a painting in Ipuy's tomb at Thebes, done about 1275 B.C. The Metropolitan Museum of Art (30.4.114)

An ancient Egyptian sandal maker sits on a three-legged stool while he cuts out a piece of leather. Copy of a tomb painting from the eighteenth dynasty, 1570 to about 1342 B.C. The Metropolitan Museum of Art (31.6.21)

A carved cedar-wood chair from the tomb of the pharaoh Tutankhamen. Thebes, the Valley of the Kings, about 1340 B.C. Photograph by Egyptian Expedition, The Metropolitan Museum of Art

Folding Egyptian stool with leather seat. From the twelfth dynasty, 1991–1786 B.C. The Metropolitan Museum of Art, Rogers Fund, 1912 (12.182. 58)

mortise and drove a wooden peg through the joint to se-
cure the two pieces of wood.

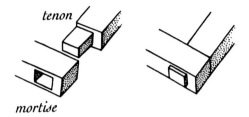

A MORTISE AND TENON JOINT

By the IV dynasty (2680–2565 B.C.) the Egyptians
were making chairs with arms. At first the arms extended out from the chair back just below the sitter's
armpits, but later they were lowered to a more comfortable elbow height. However, most Egyptian chairs continued to be made without arms.

The seats of some chairs, especially those shaped
from pieces of solid wood, were curved for ease in sitting. Sometimes cushions of linen or leather stuffed
with feathers covered the seats. None of them were upholstered, since that process was unknown to the
Egyptians.

In the New Kingdom (1570–332 B.C.) low chairs with very wide seats and short legs of only nine or so inches became popular. Perhaps the Egyptians sat cross-legged on them, like the Buddhas on Indian thrones.

Many Egyptian chairs—and stools, too—had legs that ended in realistic carvings of animal feet. These might be the hooves of a bull or horse, or the paws of a lion. No one knows why the ancient Egyptians put animal feet on their chair legs, a decorative pattern that other chairmakers have often followed in the centuries since. Perhaps it was simply because a chair, like many animals, has four legs and feet. Or perhaps the Egyptians thought the feet of a powerful animal like a lion would suggest the importance of the high official or Pharaoh who sat in the chair.

The Egyptians often painted their wooden chairs in bright colors. They also ornamented them with inlaid decorations made up of small stones or pieces of glass and pottery. The finest chairs were inlaid with ivory or ebony imported from the African lands to the south of Egypt.

Sometimes the Egyptians beat gold into a thin skin and covered a wooden chair with it. Or else they gilded parts of a chair with gold paint to make them look as if

Back panel of the Golden Throne of Tutankhamen, showing the pharaoh with his wife, Ankhesenamen. Photograph by Egyptian Expedition, The Metropolitan Museum of Art

they were made of solid gold. A good example of this is the throne of Tutankhamen, now in the Egyptian Museum in Cairo. With its gold-covered back and gilded lions' heads and paws on the legs, this throne represents the ultimate in Egyptian chair design.

Unlike the Egyptians, the ancient Greeks did not bury household furnishings with their dead. As a result, very few Greek stools and chairs have survived, except for a few examples made of bronze. However, we know what Greek seat furniture looked like from the way it is portrayed in tomb sculptures and paintings on Greek vases.

Greek houses, in both city and country, were usually built around a central courtyard. They often contained separate quarters for the men and the women, with the men's rooms located on the street side and the women's rooms at the back of the house, beyond the courtyard.

As in Egyptian homes, the stool was the most common item of seat furniture. One style had a wooden seat and four turned legs. Greek carpenters probably invented the process known as turning, and it has been an important feature of furniture design ever since. In this process, a craftsman uses a chisel to round and

A Greek gentleman sits on a stool in this sculpted relief from a marble grave monument. Greece, fourth century B.C. The Metropolitan Museum of Art, Rogers Fund, 1911 (11.100.2)

decorate a piece of wood, such as a chair leg, while it rotates between the clamps of a lathe.

Another common Greek stool was a folding model with X-shaped legs and a leather seat. Like the legs of Egyptian seat furniture, the legs of these stools often ended in carved animal paws or hooves. Carefully made, the stools reflected their owners' status. When a wealthy Greek left his house, a slave often followed behind, carrying the master's folding stool for him to sit on whenever he wanted to stop and rest.

Heavy thrones sculpted from marble served as seats for the statues of the gods in Greek temples. Similar thrones could be found in the huge open-air amphitheaters where Greek plays were performed.

Most people who attended the plays crowded onto stone seats that rose like bleachers from the central stage area to the back of the amphitheater. Only priests and other high officials were privileged to sit in the high-backed thrones. Located in the center of the amphitheater, they offered not only comfort but also the best view of the stage.

Greek women enjoyed little freedom and almost never accompanied their husbands to the theater. But in the privacy of their quarters at the back of the house, they sat in armless chairs that were among the most comfortable ever designed. This type of chair was called a *klismos*, meaning "light chair," and it was always associated with women. In fact, the poet Homer said the *klismos* had originally been made for the use of goddesses.

By the fifth century B.C. the *klismos* had become a standard item of furniture throughout Greece. The back of the chair and the back legs formed a single curve,

while the front legs curved forward to the same degree.
The back itself was topped by a slightly curved horizontal board, shaped to fit the human body and placed
at shoulder height. A leather cushion was often put on
the woven seat to make it softer.

When a Greek woman of 500 B.C. sat on a *klismos*
and let an arm drop casually over the back, she experi-
enced an ease and comfort that no chair before then

A Greek woman sits in a klismos, while two other women and a little girl holding a bird look on. Sculpted relief from a grave monument of the fourth century B.C. The Metropolitan Museum of Art, Harris Brisbane Dick Fund, 1965 (65.11.11)

had allowed—and that few other chairs would match for centuries to come.

Roman houses and seat furniture were much like those of the ancient Greeks, with one important difference. Wealthy Romans did not sit on stools, benches, or chairs when they ate a meal. Instead they lay on couches.

The Roman word for dining room came from this custom. It was *triclinium,* which meant "dining couch" in Latin—or rather "three couches," for in a typical Roman dining room there were three couches arranged around the walls. Each couch was wide enough for two or more diners, who stretched out on it and reached for food from a central table.

Their dining couches were often the most expensive pieces of furniture a Roman family owned. Many couches were made of bronze and had headboards and footboards decorated with ivory and precious metals. Thick mattresses enclosed in

A guest at a Roman funeral banquet reclines on a couch as children bring her food. Marble sculpture from the front of a burial urn. The Metropolitan Museum of Art, Fletcher Fund, 1927 (27.122.2 ab)

brightly colored sheets covered the couches, and soft pillows made them even more pleasant to lie on.

When they did not have guests, Roman families frequently ate their meals in the enclosed atriums, or courtyards, of their homes. Then only the father would recline on a couch to eat. His wife sat on a chair beside him and shared food from his table, while their children perched on stools around another table.

A Roman woman plays a cithara, an ancient form of zither, while her daughter leans on the back of her mother's chair. Wall painting from a villa in the town of Boscoreale, done between 40 and 30 B.C. The Metropolitan Museum of Art, Rogers Fund, 1903 (03.13.5)

Roman stools came in straight and cross-legged styles, like those of the Greeks. They were made of cast iron or bronze as well as wood, and most of them could be folded. The Romans carried such stools with them to the far reaches of their empire, providing models for native peoples everywhere from Britain in the West to the Black Sea region in the East.

The Romans introduced the chair to western Europe also. As in Greece, Roman chairs were usually associated with women. Some rounded chairs were made of wickerwork, like porch and garden furniture today. Other Roman chairs looked like heavier versions of the Greek *klismos*, either with or without arms. Artworks show Roman women sitting in chairs like these to nurse infants, have their hair done, play musical instruments, or simply relax.

After the collapse of the Roman Empire in the West in A.D. 476, the manufacture of elaborate stools and chairs—like so many other arts and crafts—died out in Europe. It would be hundreds of years before people there had seats as comfortable or handsome as the folding Roman stool and the Greek *klismos*. And when chair making finally did revive, it sprang up in an unexpected place.

CHAPTER THREE

A Throne for the Master

Life was hard and full of danger in Europe during the Dark Ages. That is the name we give the period between the fall of the Roman Empire and the year A.D. 1000. For more than five hundred years, rival tribes ranged across the countryside, killing their enemies and laying waste their possessions. Neither the rich nor the poor felt safe, and neither knew the security of a stable home.

Only a few places escaped the violence of the times. Among them were the Christian monasteries that could be found in every western European country. Marauding tribes usually spared the monasteries from attack because of their sacred nature. As a result, the resident monks were among the lucky few in the Dark Ages who led peaceful, settled lives.

The monks revived many crafts, including the making of furniture. That did not mean they had comfortable chairs to sit in, however. As servants of Christ, the monks were supposed to maintain a humble attitude at all times, so when they gathered for meals in the dining hall, they sat on hard wooden benches without cushions. And when they went to services in the chapel, straight-backed pews and choir stalls helped them to focus their thoughts — and to stay awake.

Two oak choir stalls with the seats folded up and the shelflike misericords clearly visible. The stalls were made in France in the fifteenth century. Note the carved heads on the misericords. Almost all misericords featured such carvings, which portrayed everything from monsters and mythical beasts to scenes from everyday life. The Metropolitan Museum of Art, Gift of J. Pierpont Morgan, 1916 (16.32.15)

The seats in the choir stalls made just one concession to comfort. Since the monks had to stand, sometimes for hours, when they chanted their prayers, the seats were designed to tip up like modern theater seats. On their undersides, placed at right angles to the upright seats, were narrow wooden shelves. During the lengthy prayers, the monks—who wore long robes—could lean or sit on the edges of the shelves without anyone knowing that they were doing so.

The shelves were called "misericords," from the Latin word meaning "pity" or "mercy." No doubt they did seem like a mercy, especially to those monks who were old or ill.

As Europe left the Dark Ages and moved into the Middle Ages, battles between rival tribes and kingdoms became less frequent and ordinary people could relax a little. But their lives were still hard.

Poor peasants in the thirteenth century often lived in cramped, windowless huts. If they had any seat furniture at all, it was usually just a couple of wooden stools. Many of these were made by boring three holes in a piece of planking, or a slice from a tree trunk, and inserting three legs in them. Wedges driven in from above held the legs in place.

Merchants and craftsmen in towns and cities did not enjoy much more in the way of comfort. Their two-story homes usually combined space for work with space for living. On the ground floor was the shop or work area, and on the floor above a single large room in which all the members of the family lived. In this room, as many as eight or ten people cooked and ate their meals, entertained their friends, and slept. Privacy, even if desired, was out of the question.

The room contained relatively little furniture, and most of the pieces served more than one purpose. There might be a stool or two by the fireplace, which was used for cooking as well as for heating. The adults in the family slept in permanent beds that were built into the corners of the room, while the children made do with pallets laid on the floor. During the day the beds were used as seats, as were the chests in which the family members stored their clothes and other possessions. At mealtime, the stools and chests took the place of chairs around the dining table.

In many medieval homes there were no chairs at all. The word "chair"—meaning a seat for one person, with four legs, a back, and often arms—didn't even enter the English language until about A.D. 1300.

If a family of modest means happened to own a chair, it was likely to be the type made by rural craftsmen all over Europe. These chairs had a wooden frame, a slatted back, and a seat of woven rushes. If the family was better off, like the merchant's household described before, their single chair was probably constructed entirely of wood. Its tall, straight back and flat, hard seat resembled those in a choir stall, but there was no

High-backed French chair from the late fifteenth or early sixteenth century. Note the locked wooden chest under the seat. The Metropolitan Museum of Art, Rogers Fund, 1907 (07.192a)

misericord built in beneath the seat. In its place there might be a chest to store linens and other items.

A loose cushion or piece of folded cloth could make the seat a little more comfortable, but there was no chance of the chair being upholstered. Furniture makers still had not developed that process.

Because they were rare, chairs became symbols of wealth and power in medieval Europe, and only the head of the household or an important guest sat in one. Since such a person was usually male, he was called a "chairman." Today the word chairman denotes someone who heads a committee or presides over a meeting. But it still reflects the importance that people once attached to chairs and those who were privileged to sit in them.

As might be expected, chairs and other types of seat furniture

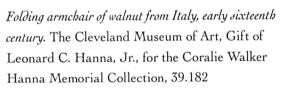

LEFT: Folding iron armchair shaped like a director's chair with a fabric seat and back. Italy, fifteenth century. The Cleveland Museum of Art, John L. Severance Fund, 49.201

Folding armchair of walnut from Italy, early sixteenth century. The Cleveland Museum of Art, Gift of Leonard C. Hanna, Jr., for the Coralie Walker Hanna Memorial Collection, 39.182

were more common in the homes of the rich during the Middle Ages, and they came in two distinct styles. Medieval kings and landowners moved frequently from castle to castle in order to keep a close eye on their holdings, so their furniture—including chairs—was either so heavy that it could be left safely in place or so light that it could be transported easily.

The lighter types of stools and chairs had seats made of animal hide and curved or straight legs that crossed in the center like the letter X. Many of them could be folded, like the X-framed folding stools of the ancient Egyptians and Romans.

The jester Calabazas stands by a folding stool with a leather seat in this portrait by the Spanish artist Diego Velázquez (1599–1660). The Cleveland Museum of Art, Leonard C. Hanna, Jr., Fund, 65.15

The heavier styles were often built into the walls of a room, like the choir stalls in monasteries. For example, long wooden benches might be part of the paneling. At dinnertime, tables would be brought in and put in front of the benches, since well-to-do medieval people usually sat on only one side of a table when eating.

Most castles had one or more heavy, thronelike chairs that were reserved for the use of the lord and his honored guests. These chairs were larger, more elaborate versions of the chairs to be found in merchants' households. Like them, the chairs of the wealthy had flat seats and tall, upright backs. In such a chair one had no choice but to sit up straight!

To make it even more thronelike, a chair of this type was often set on a platform in the great hall of a castle. A canopy projected from the chair's back, high above the head of the sitter. The canopy called attention to the person and gave him additional prominence.

One of the most famous thronelike medieval chairs is Great Britain's coronation chair, which can be seen in Westminster Abbey in London. Made to the order of King Edward I in the thirteenth century, the chair was designed to be cast in bronze but was constructed of oak instead. The kings and queens of England are still crowned while sitting in the eight-hundred-year-old coronation chair.

After the Renaissance in art and learning began in Italy about 1400, life in Europe gradually became more stable. Noblemen no longer felt a need to move their

Great Britain's coronation chair in Westminster Abbey, made about 1296 for King Edward I. A platform was placed beneath the seat to hold the Stone of Scone, on which Scottish kings had been crowned for over three hundred years. King Edward brought the stone back to England after defeating the Scots in battle. The four gilded lions on which the chair rests are later additions, probably from the time of Queen Elizabeth I. The Bettmann Archive

possessions from one house or castle to another. They now sought more permanent furniture that would remain in one place, but it didn't have to be built in.

As the Renaissance spread northward, a prosperous new middle class of merchants and traders came into being in the cities of Holland and other countries. These people were well enough off to maintain homes separate from their businesses. Their dwellings usually contained a series of rooms rather than a single large one, and the furniture in the rooms — whether chests, beds, or chairs — served one purpose rather than several.

Benches and stools were still the rule in poorer European homes, but the chair had become the preferred seat among well-to-do families. However, the new-style chairs were very different from those of the medieval period. Sometimes they weren't even called chairs.

A prosperous Flemish merchant sits in a straight-backed armchair, his young son standing beside him. Etching and engraving by Michael Sweerts (1618–1664). The Cleveland Museum of Art, Gift of The Print Club of Cleveland in honor of Dr. Sherman E. Lee, 82.177

Often in European homes, after the dinner dishes were cleared away, people would sit on side chairs around the dining table to play musical instruments and sing. Engraving titled "The Sense of Hearing," by French artist Abraham Bosse (1602–1676). The Metropolitan Museum of Art, Harris Brisbane Dick Fund, 1926 (26.49.22)

Up till then, all European chairs had come with arms, but many of the new models did not have them. Consequently, they were known in England as "backstools"—stools with backs attached to them.

Backstools were especially popular with women who wore farthingales, the hoopskirts that were fashionable in the sixteenth and seventeenth centuries. The women could sit comfortably on armless backstools, whereas it was hard to fit their farthingales into chairs with arms.

Eventually the names of chairs changed again. Chairs with arms became known, naturally enough, as

A Dutch woman in a farthingale stands near one of the new-style upholstered armchairs. It is wide enough to accommodate her hoopskirt. Oil painting by Gerard ter Borch (1617–1681). The Cleveland Museum of Art, The Elizabeth Severance Prentiss Collection, 44.93

armchairs, while backstools were called side chairs. This was because upper-class people now took their meals in a room used only for dining, and chairs without arms could be placed more easily along the sides of the dining table.

Whatever they were called—backstools or armchairs or side chairs—Renaissance chairs were much more comfortable than their predecessors. For the first time, craftsmen began to upholster chairs. They did this by stuffing pads with rolls of horsehair and other materials, covering them with fabric or leather, and then attaching the pads to the seats and backs of chairs with tacks.

Padded chairs quickly became the rage. In the late 1500s an Englishman, Sir John Harington, wrote: "The fashion of cushioned chayres is taken up in every merchant's house." But these early examples of upholstered chairs still had drawbacks in terms of comfort. The stuffing in the pads was often thin, and the flat seats and backs continued to resist the curves of the human body.

That was soon to change. Expanding trade with the Far East included furniture, and merchants brought back chairs from India and China that would revolutionize European chair design.

CHAPTER FOUR

Barbarian Couches

For centuries, most people in India had sat or squatted on the floor. But after the Portuguese opened up sea routes to India in the fifteenth and sixteenth centuries, traders from Portugal, the Netherlands, and England settled in the major Indian port cities. The traders were chiefly interested in such commodities as tea, spices, textiles, and ivory, but they also taught the Indians how to make chairs in the European style.

Why have chairs made in far-off India for shipment back to European markets? Then as now, the main reason was cost. An English lord, Sir Dudley North, put it plainly in a book written in 1691: "As much labor or manufacture may be had in India for two pence as in England for a shilling [twelve pence]."

While basically following European models, the Indians introduced some innovations in chair design. One of these was the use of woven caning for chair backs and seats. Europeans liked the caned panels because they were light and flexible, and the many small openings in them allowed air to circulate. They also believed that the panels would discourage termites and other vermin that might breed in chairs made of solid wood.

Even bigger changes in chair design resulted from the samples of Chinese chairs that European merchants imported.

It may seem surprising that the Chinese of the seventeenth century sat in chairs, since their neighbors, the Japanese, were accustomed to sitting on the floor. And, in fact, the ancient Chinese did also. Until about A.D. 200, they reclined and slept on low, built-in platforms called *k'ang*s. In northern China, where the winters could be extremely cold, the *k'ang*s were heated with flues that reached out from stoves and ran beneath the platforms.

Woven mats and sometimes carpets covered *k'ang*s in both northern and southern China. Usually a *k'ang* also had a low central table at which the Chinese sat cross-legged to write letters and eat their meals.

Then, sometime in the second century A.D., chairs first appeared in China. No one knows exactly where the chairs came from, but they were probably transported all the way from Greece or Rome across the deserts and mountains of the northern trade route. Supporting this notion is the early Chinese name for a chair—"barbarian couch." At the time, the Chinese thought of all people from the west as barbarians.

By the T'ang dynasty (A.D. 618–906) there was already a sharp difference between the furniture found in ordinary Chinese homes and the pieces made for high officials and members of the emperor's household. Most common people

The Chinese God of Wealth is shown sitting in a chair with a curved back and dragon's heads at the ends of the arms. Porcelain figure from the late seventeenth century. The Metropolitan Museum of Art, Bequest of John D. Rockefeller, Jr., 1960 (60.200.11)

sat on simple wooden stools or reclined on *k'ang*s as their ancestors had in earlier centuries.

More elaborate stools, with loose, tasseled cushions on them, filled the rooms in wealthier homes. Such stools were considered perfect seats for women, since they displayed the curve of a woman's back and shoulders—a mark of beauty in T'ang times—while allowing her to sit modestly.

The homes of the wealthy also contained numerous chairs. They ranged in style from heavy armchairs, with thick, embroidered cushions on them for use in winter, to lighter styles, with backs and seats of bamboo and rattan for summer. And, like the chairs in medieval Europe, they were usually reserved for men.

The Chinese had special customs connected with chairs. For example, they thought it was impolite to offer a gentleman a chair that another had sat in recently. Different chair coverings indicated the rank and profession of the sitter. A rich silk or brocade would be spread over the chair of a government official, while tiger skins were the rule for military leaders.

The position of the chair in a room added to its importance. The farther away it was from the entrance, the more honor it conferred on the sitter. A chair directly opposite the entrance occupied the most favorable location of all.

To the Chinese, informal furniture arrangements showed bad taste, and they preferred to set as much furniture as possible against the walls of a room. Two chairs, facing outward and with a small, low table between them, often formed a three-piece group designed as a unit. Such groupings can still be found in Chinese offices and government buildings today.

Because Chinese floors, even in palaces, were made of wood or polished bricks and were usually not covered with rugs, they often got cold and damp—especially in winter. So Chinese craftsmen made chairs higher than those in the west and put a low rung between the front legs to serve as a footrest. With it, a Chinese gentleman could keep his feet comfortably above the floor when he relaxed in his favorite chair on a chilly winter evening.

A unique feature of Chinese furniture, including chairs, was the complete absence of nails and pegs in its construction. Like the ancient Egyptians, the Chinese relied on mortise and tenon joints instead, but used a small amount of glue rather than pegs to help hold them together. Chinese craftsmen concealed the joints so skillfully that they were almost invisible.

When trade with Europe expanded in the sixteenth century, the Chinese were making a wide variety of chairs. Some closely resembled the chairs of medieval

Wooden Chinese chair with footrest in front.
The Metropolitan Museum of Art,
Seymour Fund, 1967 (67.58)

A group of high Chinese officials at a banquet. The coverings draped over the men's chairs indicate their rank, and the platform on which the host (back to viewer) sits shows that he is the most important person in the room. Nineteenth-century angraving from the Kubler Collection. Photo by Ken Pelka, The Cooper-Hewitt Museum of the Smithsonian Institution

Europe. They had boxlike bases, tall, straight backs, and rigid arms. But others were more comfortable than any chairs seen in the West since the days of the ancient Greeks.

One style was probably the world's first reclining chair. It had a headrest that tilted back and a piece that extended from the seat so the sitter could stretch out his legs. Because the chair encouraged sprawling, it was popularly known as a "drunken lord's chair."

Far more common—and especially appealing to European customers—were the Chinese chairs with curved backs. The curve usually did not end with the back, but continued on into the arms. Not since the Greek *klismos* had a chair been so well suited to the contours of the human body.

But even though these Chinese chair designs made a strong impression in Europe, and led to the manufacture of more comfortable chairs there, Europeans were reluctant to abandon the old idea of the chair as a symbol of power and authority. For them, that was still a chair's most important value. This notion would be carried to its furthest extreme by King Louis XIV of France in his palace at Versailles.

CHAPTER FIVE

Who Gets to Sit in a Chair?

King Louis XIV, who ruled France from 1643 to 1715, once said, "I am the State," and his palace at Versailles seemed to prove it.

Louis and his architects planned the palace on a grand scale for political rather than artistic reasons. The king wanted to keep an eye on the powerful French nobles who, he feared, might plot against him. So he made it clear that any noble who hoped to win his favor must come to Versailles and stay at the palace for long periods.

To accommodate all the guests, Versailles grew into an enormous structure over 600 yards long on the side facing the gardens. At any given time, thousands of people lived at the palace. Besides the king and members of his family, there were countless princes and princesses, dukes and duchesses, and more than five hundred servants.

With so many nobles gathered in one place, marks of status assumed tremendous importance. Dukes competed for the privilege of standing in the king's bedchamber when he woke up in the morning, and again when he went to bed at night. And everyone at Versailles had to observe strict rules of rank and position when it came to the use of seat furniture.

In some rooms nobody but Louis could sit, and his bedroom contained no chairs at all. When the king received visitors there, they remained standing while he sat on the edge of the bed.

In the palace's large public rooms, only Louis himself ever sat in an armchair. His queen, other members of the royal family, and the king's closest associates sat in chairs without arms. High-ranking nobles were permitted to sit on cushioned, three-legged stools called *tabourets*. Lesser nobles had to make do with unpadded folding stools.

Occasionally permission to sit on a stool was granted to someone whose rank did not merit it. But this was considered an exceptional favor, and was for one time only.

An inventory of palace furnishings taken after Louis's death listed 1,325 stools of various types. That may sound like a huge number until it's compared with

Even very young French kings wore the robes of state and sat in thronelike chairs. Here is King Louis XV as a child, painted by Hyacinthe Rigaud (1659–1743). The Metropolitan Museum of Art, Purchase, Bequest of Mary Westmore Shively in memory of her husband, Henry L. Shively, M.D., 1960 (60.6)

the population of Versailles at the time. Upward of 5,000 people were staying at the palace, which meant that most of them spent their days standing up. Only at night, in the privacy of their rooms, could they enjoy the luxury of sitting.

Walnut armchair from the time of Louis XIV. Note needlepoint coverings on the seat and back. The Metropolitan Museum of Art, Bequest of Benjamin Altman, 1913 (14.40.782)

While they would never dare to sit in a chair in the presence of the king, many members of the French nobility had armchairs like his in their own townhouses and palaces. And so did the upper classes in other European countries, from Italy to England.

The home furnishings of the day reflected the baroque style that was popular in art and architecture throughout Europe. This style emphasized ornamentation and relied on curved rather than straight lines. Baroque chairs often had wooden backs carved in floral or abstract designs and richly upholstered seats. Some backs featured caned central panels, like those in Chinese chairs.

Whether in a London townhouse or a Roman palace, baroque furniture was always arranged in formal patterns. Chairs without arms were usually lined up close to one another along the walls of a room. Servants might bring them out into the middle and set them around a table for a card game or a meal. But after it was over, they would immediately put them back against the walls.

A key feature in many baroque interiors was the so-called "Canopy of State." It was an updated version of the thronelike chairs in which medieval kings and nobles had received visitors, administered justice, and even eaten their meals.

Like those chairs, the baroque "Canopy of State" consisted of three parts—a raised platform with an elaborate chair on it and a canopy high above. There were strict rules for the size and dimensions of the canopy and the backcloth that hung down from it, based on the rank of the sitter. For example, the backcloth behind a king's chair reached all the way to the

Christian VIII, King of Denmark from 1839–1848, sits on his throne under a Canopy of State. Beside him is his queen, Caroline Amalie. Note that her Canopy of State is less elaborate than the king's, and the backcloth behind her throne in narrower. Portrait by Dobbelt, The Royal Danish Collections at Rosenborg Palace, Copenhagen

floor, while a duke's backcloth stopped two thirds of the way down, and an earl's was shorter still.

Life in France was less formal during the reign of Louis XV (1715–1774). The new king believed in pleasure and liked to relax in comfortable chairs.

Influenced by Chinese designs, French craftsmen began to make chairs with slanted backs and curved arms. The padded back of one of these new-style armchairs was lower than those in earlier models. The seat was wider, and the arms did not extend all the way to the front of the seat.

These features were designed to accommodate the women's fashions of the period. The set-back armrests made room for their broad, hooped skirts, and the low backs did not interfere with their elaborate hairstyles. But men liked them, too. In such an armchair, a sitter could turn easily from one side to the other, lean on the padded arms, and talk directly with his or her neighbor in a way that had not been possible before.

Side chairs continued to line the walls of reception rooms in wealthy homes, but chairs were now placed in less rigid arrangements. A matching pair of armchairs often faced each other on either side of a fireplace. Other armchairs were scattered about the drawing rooms and bedrooms of upper-class homes. Light in weight, they were called "running chairs" because they could be moved quickly and easily from one location to another as the need arose.

Most running chairs had upholstered seats and backs, but none of the seats contained springs. That method of construction had not been invented yet. However, the upholstery was much thicker and more comfortable than the padding in earlier chairs.

Chairmakers still used horsehair, sometimes mixed with straw and swamp moss, for the padding, but they now gave it a domed shape. This meant the center of the

Three French aristocrats seated in "running chairs" have a conversation in a boudoir. Print by Jean-Michel Moreau le Jeune (1741–1814). The Metropolitan Museum of Art, Harris Brisbane Dick Fund, 1933 (33.6.30)

seat would take most of the person's weight and the front edge would be less likely to cut into his or her thighs.

A French craftsman removes the horsehair stuffing from the back of a chair before re-upholstering it. Plate from Denis Diderot's Encyclopédie, *Paris, 1751–1772.* The New York Public Library

On top of the padding the chairmakers stitched a layer of linen. Then they covered the seat, back, and arms with fabric. In the 1700s the most common upholstery fabric was needlepoint, an embroidery of woolen threads on canvas. It had a rough surface that helped to keep the sitter from sliding forward in a chair.

Needlepoint could also be worked into elaborate designs of floral arrangements or scenes from mythology. If such a design appeared on a chair back, it was usually protected by a flap of plain cloth. When the chair was not in use, the flap hung down behind the back, where it was out of sight. But it could be pulled quickly over the expensive needlepoint if a fashionable man or woman wearing a powdered wig decided to sit in the chair.

All of Europe tended to follow the furniture styles that were set in France during the reigns of Louis XIV and Louis XV. In fact, upholstered armchairs were known in England as "French chairs."

However, English chairmakers soon began to create bold new styles of their own. And those styles were carried to colonial America, where they inspired further advances in chair design.

CHAPTER SIX

Chairs for Everyone

A great demand for chairs of all types arose in England in the 1700s. Special chairs were even being made for young children for the first time. Some of them had steps for the child to climb up and—like today's highchairs—a bar across the arms to prevent the sitter from falling out.

To meet the demand for chairs, teams of craftsmen combined their skills to produce them in cabinetmaking shops. The *joiner* cut and shaped the wooden frame of the chair and joined the pieces together. The *carver* executed any special decorations on the back, arms, or legs. The *painter* and *gilder* added color and gold leaf when required. And finally the *upholsterer* provided the padded seat and back if they were part of the chair's design.

One of the best known of eighteenth-century English chairmakers was Thomas Chippendale (1718–1779).

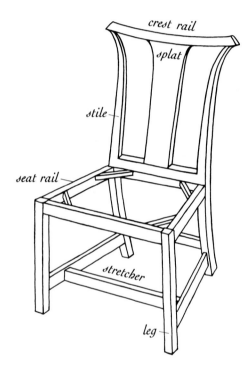

crest rail

splat

stile

seat rail

stretcher

leg

THE PARTS OF A CHAIR

He had many wealthy clients, and his cabinetmaking firm was one of the most respected in London.

In 1754 Chippendale published an illustrated catalogue, *Gentleman's and Cabinetmaker's Director*. It contained 160 engravings of his furniture designs, many of them for chairs, and included the exact dimensions of each chair's height, width, and depth. The dimensions could be altered, Chippendale wrote, "according to the Bigness of the Rooms the chairs are intended for."

In his catalogue, Chippendale used the same words to describe the various parts of a chair that craftsmen employ today. A *stretcher* was a wooden crosspiece that joined any two legs of the chair and gave them added stability. The *seat rail* united all four legs and provided a frame for the seat.

The two vertical elements that rose from the seat or legs and helped to support the back were the *stiles*. The horizontal piece that joined the tops of the stiles was the *crest rail*. The central panel, narrow or wide, in the chair's back had an odd-sounding name. It was called the *splat*.

Chippendale specialized in side chairs, and he emphasized the back of the chair in his designs. There was an economic reason for this. Due to the high cost of needlepoint and other upholstery coverings, many of Chippendale's middle-class customers could not afford to have chairs with padded backs as well as seats. So Chippendale made the wooden backs of his chairs as comfortable and attractive as possible. He pierced and carved the splats in intricate designs of scrolls and leaves, or latticework in the "Chinese style."

Chippendale often used mahogany in his chairs. An extremely hard wood, mahogany was first known as "Jamaica wood" because it came from Jamaica and other islands in the West Indies. This dark, lustrous wood could be carved easily, and it produced chairs that combined strength and lightness.

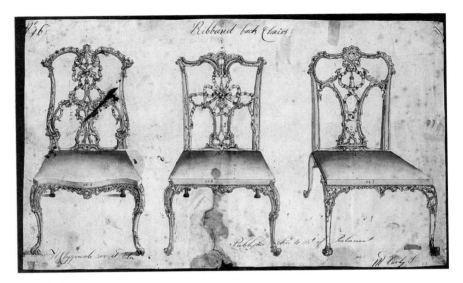

Drawing by Thomas Chippendale from his book Gentleman's and Cabinetmaker's Director. The Metropolitan Museum of Art, Rogers Fund, 1972 (1972.581)

Although many of Chippendale's chairs had gently curved backs that accommodated the human figure, most people of the time sat up straight in them. The men did not want to disturb their wigs by leaning back, and the women were forced into an upright posture by their tightly laced corsets.

Chippendale's furniture catalogue proved to be immensely popular, and inspired other English chair designers to compile similar books. The first of these was George Hepplewhite, whose book *The Cabinet-Maker and Upholsterer's Guide* was published by his widow in 1788, two years after his death.

In the preface, Hepplewhite stated his chief goal as a furniture maker: "To unite elegance and utility, and blend the useful with the agreeable, has ever been considered a difficult, but an honorable task. . . ." His book included a beautiful series of designs for chairs with upholstered seats and oval-, heart-, and shield-shaped backs.

The third great English chairmaker of the eighteenth century was Thomas Sheraton (1751–1806). A deeply religious man, he wrote in his manual *Cabinet Maker and Upholsterer's Drawing-Book*: "Though I am employed in racking my invention to design fine and pleasing furniture, I can be well content to sit on a wooden bottom chair myself, provided I can but have common food and clothing wherewith to pass through this life in peace."

Side chair in the Hepplewhite style, made in Salem, Massachusetts, between 1790 and 1799. The Metropolitan Museum of Art, Lee Fund, 1937 (37.81.1)

Mahogany side chair in the style of Thomas Sheraton made about 1800. The Metropolitan Museum of Art, Gift of the Members of the Committee of the Bertha King Bernard Memorial Fund, 1946 (46.67.99)

Sheraton's own chair designs were anything but common. They had a graceful delicacy, and many of the backs featured carvings of lyres, urns, and other objects associated with ancient Greece and Rome.

These chairs of Sheraton's reflected the neoclassical style that was popular in Europe at the time. Pompeii and the neighboring Roman city of Herculaneum had been excavated earlier in the eighteenth century, and the discoveries made there had helped to spark a new interest in the art and architecture of the ancient — or "classical" — world.

Sheraton's book, like those of Chippendale and Hepplewhite, circulated widely in colonial America as well as England. The books were the forerunners of today's do-it-yourself manuals. Following the instructions in them, a craftsman anywhere could make copies of the latest in English chair designs.

Not all chair styles of the time originated in the workshops of London, however. Some of the most popular designs had much humbler origins. One of these — which is still being manufactured today — was the Windsor chair.

No one knows exactly how the Windsor chair got its name. Some say that King George III of England found several chairs of this type when he sought shelter in a cottage near Windsor Castle during a rainstorm. The king thought the chairs were so comfortable that he ordered some to be made for his own use. He dubbed them "Windsor chairs," and thereafter that was what they were always called.

Whether that story is true or not, the Windsor chair was certainly comfortable. Made entirely of wood, it had a solid seat carved with twin depressions to fit the rear end of the sitter. The semicircular back was formed of wooden spindles that rose from the seat to a curved yoke, called a *bow*, that also served as an armrest.

In some Windsor chairs, a second set of spindles rose to another curved bow or to a horizontal piece of wood called a *comb*. This type of Windsor chair provided even more support to the sitter's back.

Easy to make, attractive, and inexpensive, Windsor chairs could soon be found in London townhouses as well as country cottages. They were also shipped to Boston, Philadelphia, and other cities in colonial America. There, local craftsmen developed a low-backed Windsor chair that became extremely popular. It was used to furnish a wide variety of places, from private homes to taverns to public buildings. Among the latter was the State House in Philadelphia, where the delegates to the Continental Congress in 1778 all sat in low-backed Windsor chairs.

Another type of chair

Windsor armchair, made in America between 1750 and 1775. The Metropolitan Museum of Art, Gift of Mrs. Russell Sage, 1909 (10.125.269)

Delegates to the Second Continental Congress, including Benjamin Franklin, relax in Windsor chairs. Detail from an engraving titled "The Congress Voting Independence" after the painting of the same name by Edward Savage. The Historical Society of Pennsylvania

that found favor in both England and colonial America was an upholstered armchair with wings on either side of the high back. The wings surrounded a sitter and made him or her feel protected. They also shielded the sitter from cold drafts or the direct heat of open fires.

Wing chairs were so comfortable that they soon became known as "easy chairs." They were called "grandfather chairs," too, because many old people used them. A wing chair would often be placed next to the bed in an upstairs bedchamber, where an old person could get to it quickly and easily.

Indoor plumbing was unknown in the eighteenth century, so many wing chairs contained removable chamber pots beneath their seat cushions. For people whose feet ached from gout, a common disease at the time, craftsmen made upholstered "gouty stools" to accompany their wing chairs.

Chairmaking was a specialized profession in the cities of colonial America. A young man became an apprentice chairmaker at fifteen and by the age of twenty-one was judged ready to practice his craft. He would then hire himself out to master chairmakers for the next few years until he had accumulated enough money and experience to go into business for himself. At that point, he took on apprentices of his own and the cycle would be repeated.

Early American craftsmen developed several unique chairs, among them the rocking chair. Its invention has been credited—along with so many other things—to Benjamin Franklin. According to the story, Franklin turned his attention to designing a more comfortable chair sometime between 1760 and 1770. He experimented with several different designs before he got the

The aged Mrs. Anna Dummer Powell sat in a wing chair for this portrait by the American artist John Singleton Copley (1737–1815). The Cleveland Museum of Art, Gift of Ellery Sedgwick, Jr., in memory of Mabel Cabot Sedgwick, 80.202

Mother sits in a rocking chair to rock the baby in this painting titled "Just Moved" by the American artist Henry Mosler (1841–1920). The Metropolitan Museum of Art, Arthur Hoppock Hearn Fund, 1962 (62.80)

idea of linking the front and back legs of a Windsor chair with two curved pieces of iron. Thus the rocking chair was born.

The new chair caught on quickly, and craftsmen made improvements in it, replacing the heavy metal rockers with lighter ones of wood. Among the chair's most enthusiastic users were young mothers, who welcomed it as a laborsaving device. Now, for the first time, the mothers could rock their babies while relaxing a little themselves.

By the early 1800s a rocking chair or two could be found in almost every American parlor, and on many front porches, too. Children and grownups alike enjoyed sitting in them, and if no adults were around, a child would often try to see how high he or she could get the rockers to go.

Plain rocking chairs were usually made of birch or elm wood. Many had

Fancy American rocking chair of maple, pine, and mahogany, with painted decorations. The Metropolitan Museum of Art, Gift of Mr. Arnold Skromme, 1971

woven rush seats and what were called "ladder backs."
These were formed of horizontal wooden slats that
linked the stiles of the chair like the rungs of a ladder.
There were also more expensive rocking chairs made of
mahogany, with elaborately carved backs.

A British visitor to the United States in 1838, who
had not seen a rocking chair before the trip, wrote to a
friend back home: "In America, it is considered a com-
pliment to give the stranger the rocking chair as a seat;
and when there is more than one kind in the house, the
stranger is always presented with the best."

Some manufacturers advertised that rocking chairs
were good for one's health. They said they were "a useful invention for invalids and others," and claimed that
rocking in one aided the digestion. The ads even called
them "digestive chairs." Most Americans needed no
special persuasion to buy a rocker, however. They liked
rockers for their own sake, whether or not the chairs
were medically beneficial.

One type of rocking chair stood out above all others
in terms of beauty and craftsmanship. This was the
rocker produced—along with other chair styles—by
the members of a small and often persecuted religious
sect: the Shakers.

CHAPTER SEVEN

From Simple to Overstuffed

"Set not your hearts on worldly objects," the Shakers said, "but let this be your labor—to keep a spiritual sense always." The Shakers tried to follow that rule in everything they did, from the way they lived their lives to the furniture they made in their workshops.

The Shaker movement had its beginnings at a Quaker revival meeting in England in 1747. Some of the Quakers who attended the meeting were so filled with religious emotion that they began to tremble and shake. They became known as the "Shaking Quakers" but did not exert any real influence until a woman named Ann Lee joined the group.

Mother Lee—as her followers called her—claimed that she embodied the female element in Christ's nature, and the Shakers soon recognized her as their leader. Fleeing persecution in England, Mother Lee led a band of eight Shakers to New York State, and in 1776

Shaker bedroom from the North family dwelling, New York State, about 1835. All of the furniture in the room was made by Shaker craftsmen. The Metropolitan Museum of Art, Emily C. Chadbourne Fund, 1972 (1972.187.1)

they founded a colony at Watervliet, a town near Albany.

Mother Lee sought to establish a new breed of human beings who would live without violence, greed, or lust. Shaker men and women enjoyed sexual equality, but they could not marry, have children, own private property, or maintain contact with the outside world.

The Shaker movement gained many converts, and by the 1780s there were Shaker communities in Massachusetts, Connecticut, New Hampshire, and Maine as well as New York. Mother Lee died in 1784, but the movement went on, establishing new communities in the frontier states of Kentucky, Ohio, and Indiana. By 1825 the Shaker population had grown to almost twenty-five hundred.

Life in a Shaker community centered on the "family." Each community consisted of two or three families, and the larger communities had five or more. A family was made up of anywhere from a few dozen to a hundred members, often unrelated, who occupied a single large building. The men, known as brothers, and the women, who were called sisters, lived dormitory style in separate sections of the building. Children who came to the community with their parents or as charity cases stayed in boys' and girls' houses with adult caretakers of the same sex.

Each Shaker family had its own workshops. In them the family members spent six days a week laboring at a wide range of trades, including furniture making. Their products met most of their own needs, and the rest were sold to supplement the community's income based on farming.

Different communities specialized in different manufactures. For instance, the New Lebanon, New York, community gained renown for its chairs. It even issued a mail-order catalogue that pictured available styles and listed their prices.

The Shakers believed that simplicity and uniformity were evidence of perfection, and their chair designs reflected this. Made of maple or birch, most Shaker chairs had rounded legs, three slats across the back, and seats of woven cotton or woolen tape. The chairs slanted backward at an angle that was comfortable for sitting, and many were equipped with rockers.

The Shakers often painted their chairs a bright yellow and criss-crossed red and blue tapes in the seats. Otherwise, the chairs had no decorations and needed none. The chairs' beauty came from the purity of their forms, the harmony of their various parts, and the obvious care that had been taken by those who made them. For the Shakers always heeded Mother Lee's instruction: "Do all your work as though you had a thousand years to live, and as you would if you knew you must die tomorrow."

Shaker chairs were prized in their own time and are valued even more today, when the Shaker movement has almost entirely died out. The chairs also helped to set a standard for later designers. But they were by no means typical of the chairs being made in the

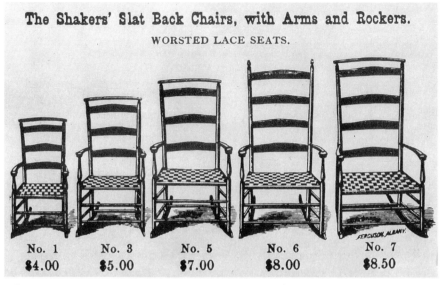

The Shakers' Slat Back Chairs, with Arms and Rockers.

WORSTED LACE SEATS.

| No. 1 | No. 3 | No. 5 | No. 6 | No. 7 |
| $4.00 | $5.00 | $7.00 | $8.00 | $8.50 |

Advertisement for chairs from a nineteenth-century Shaker mail-order catalogue. The New York Public Library

early nineteenth century. In fact, the clean-lined simplicity of Shaker chairs was more the exception than the rule.

In France, the emperor Napoleon's identification with the rulers of ancient Rome had led to the so-called Empire style in dress and furniture. Empire chairs resembled the elegant seat furniture of Greece and Rome and were narrower than the upholstered chairs that had been popular at the French court a century earlier. This was partly because women had stopped wearing hoopskirts and now appeared in straight-lined dresses modeled on classical Greek garments.

Some Empire chairs were made to fill special needs of the time. One was the "chair for an officer," with the arms missing but the front supports for them still present. A uniformed military man could sit in this chair and hold onto the supports without having to remove the saber that hung from his belt.

Empire styles spread to other European countries and to the United States, where they were called Federal styles in honor of the new nation's federal form of government. A famous American designer of Federal furniture was Duncan Phyfe, whose family had emigrated to America from Scotland. After serving as an apprentice cabinetmaker in Albany, Duncan moved to New York City, changed the spelling of his last name from Fife to the fancier Phyfe, and went into business for himself.

Federal side chair from the workshop of Duncan Phyfe, made about 1800. The Metropolitan Museum of Art, Gift of the Family of Mr. and Mrs. Andrew Varick Stout, in their memory, 1965 (65.188.2)

One of his best-known Federal chair designs looked very much like the ancient Greek *klismos*.

Nineteenth-century inventors applied their ingenuity to chair design in a variety of ways. Some created wheelchairs for those unable to walk—but the vehicles were not called wheelchairs at first. They were known instead as Bath chairs, after the English health resort where aged and infirm visitors used them to get around.

The typical Bath chair had two large wheels in back and a smaller one in front. A younger relative or servant pushed the chair by means of a horizontal bar at the rear, while the occupant steered it with a handle connected to the front wheel. The seat was often upholstered, and a canvas hood could be raised over the chair in bad weather.

As the nineteenth century wore on, manufacturers put the larger wheels in front and attached hand rims to them so that the sitter could propel the chair by himself or herself. At about the same time, people began to call the chairs wheelchairs. They were first used widely in the United States for sick and wounded soldiers during the Civil War.

Another nineteenth-century invention revolution-

Before bath chairs or wheelchairs were invented, people who could not walk were often pulled about in makeshift chairs on wheels like this one. Print titled "A Paraleytic Woman," by the French artist Théodore Géricault (1791–1824). The Cleveland Museum of Art, Seventy-fifth Anniversary Gift of The Print Club of Cleveland, 90.49

ized the design and manufacture of upholstered chairs. This was the coiled metal spring, for which first an Austrian upholsterer and then an English inventor obtained patents in the 1820s.

When chairmakers combined a number of the springs in a frame and covered the frame with upholstery, they produced a much more comfortable seat

IMPROVED INVALID CARRIAGES, SELF-PROPELLING CHAIRS, AND BATH CHAIRS.

No. 12025.

No. 12023. Invalid Carriage, medium size, upholstered in American cloth, with apron complete, £6 each.
No. 12024. As No. 12023, but with guide handle, £7 10/ each.
No. 12025. As No. 12024, see engraving, £9 each.
No. 12026. As No. 12024, but superior cloth lined, £10 10/ each.

No. 12034. Wicker Invalid Chairs, lined in best leather, small size, 80/; middle size, £5; full size, £6 each.
These chairs are made with good bodies of the best buff osiers, they are substantial and well finished, best coach wheels, and steel elliptic springs, good frame, guide rod, and duck leather aprons.

No. 12027.

No. 12027. Bath Chair, upholstered in best duck leather, £14 10/ each.
No. 12028. Bath Chair, upholstered in morocco leather, £16 10/ each.
These chairs are of the best description, with either solid side panels or rails as engraving.
Best knuckle jointed hood, 60/ extra.

No. 12029.

No. 12029. Improved Invalid Carriage, small size, to suit a child from six to twelve years of age, 90/ each.

No. 12030. As No. 12029, but middle size, to suit youth from twelve to sixteen years of age, £5 10/ each.
No. 12031. As No. 12029, but large, to suit an ordinary sized person, £6 10/ each.
No. 12032. As No. 12029, extra large, to suit a tall or heavy person, £7 15/ each.
If upholstered in good carriage cloth or rep and carriage leather apron, 40/ and 50/ each extra. This carriage being especially low the invalid can get in or out without exertion.

No. 12035. Wicker Invalid Chairs, unlined, small size, 50/; middle size, 66/; full size, 75/ each. With best carriage wheels and strong frame body, either buff or japanned.

No. 12036. Improved Invalid Carriage, one of the most comfortable made, with first-class wheels, best steel springs, guide rod, neatly painted and upholstered with best duck leather, small size, 90/; middle size, £6 10/; large size, £7 5/; extra large, £9 each.
If upholstered in carriage cloth and leather apron, 40/ and 50/ each extra. Knuckle-jointed Hoods, 50/ and 65/ extra.

SILBER & FLEMING,
Wood Street,
LONDON, E.C.

No. 12033. Self-propelling Chair, made and finished in the most substantial manner, from £7 15/ to £9 15/ each.

Nineteenth-century British advertisement for bath chairs and wheelchairs. Picture Library, The Cooper-Hewitt Museum of the Smithsonian Institution

A soldier wounded during the American Civil War sits in a self-propelled wheelchair at Carver Hospital, Washington, D.C. Detail from a photograph by Matthew Brady. The Brady Collection, National Archives

than the padded type that had been in use for hundreds of years. By the 1840s easy chairs with springs had become all the rage in America as well as Europe, and their thick upholstery had earned them the name "overstuffed chairs."

The biggest customers for the new chairs were members of the rising middle class of merchants, bankers, doctors, and other professionals. Eager to display their wealth, these people filled their living rooms, parlors, studies, and even bedrooms with overstuffed chairs. The chairs' wooden frames might be carved in some past style—Gothic, Tudor, or baroque—but all the cushioned seats were sure to contain springs.

Overstuffed chairs encouraged sitters to relax in them, but some critics felt that young men took this much too far. In a book published in 1842, an Englishman with the unusual name of Orlando Sabertash wrote: "I must here denounce as a breach of good manners the way young gentlemen lounge in graceless attitudes on sofas and armchairs. All these vile and distorted postures must be reserved for the privacy of the library, and should never be displayed in the presence of gentlemen, and still less in that of ladies."

But most people had only good things to say about

the chairs. An English poet, Eliza Cook, expressed the feelings of many on both sides of the Atlantic when she wrote in 1838:

I love it, I love it; and who shall dare
To chide me for loving that old arm-chair?

A girl and her little dog loll in two overstuffed chairs. Oil painting by the American artist Mary Cassatt (1844–1926). National Gallery of Art, Washington, Collection of Mr. and Mrs. Paul Mellon, 1983.1.18

A third nineteenth-century invention led to perhaps the most radical change of all in chair design. Like the coiled spring, it originated in Austria. There, in about 1830, a young craftsman named Michael Thonet began to experiment with new techniques of making furniture that involved neither carving nor joining. Thonet's goal: to produce simple, high-quality designs efficiently and at a low cost.

In Thonet's time, chairs were expensive because the curved parts—the arms, the legs, the backs, or all three—had to be laboriously and wastefully carved from individual blocks of wood. The parts could be made by joining two or more pieces of wood together, but that method weakened them as a whole.

Thonet knew that shipbuilders softened the timbers for ships' hulls with water and heat so they could curve them, and he decided to try a similar approach with his chairs. He took thin strips of a readily available wood like beech and glued them together in layers in such a way that the grain of one strip ran in the opposite direction to the grain of the next. This process is called *lamination*. After that, he applied steam to the laminated wood so that he could bend it into the desired shape.

Through further experimentation, Thonet discovered that he could use strong metal straps and forms to bend and twist solid pieces of wood. Now he was able to mold the backs and arms of his chairs in an almost

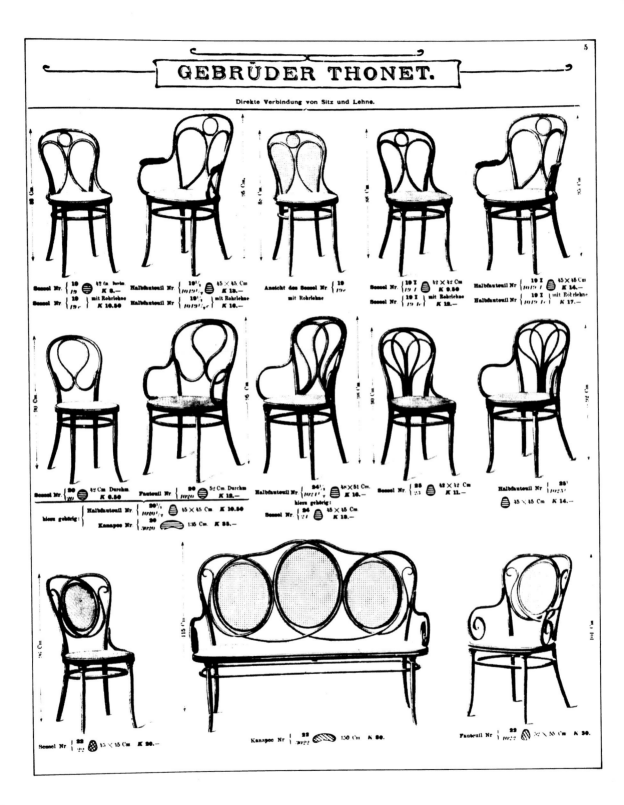

GEBRÜDER THONET.

Direkte Verbindung von Sitz und Lehne.

Sessel Nr. 19 · 42 Cm Durchm. · K 9.—
Sessel Nr. 19 c · mit Rohrlehne · K 10.50

Halbfauteuil Nr. 19½ · 45 × 45 Cm · K 13.—
Halbfauteuil Nr. 19½ c · mit Rohrlehne · K 16.—

Ansicht des Sessel Nr. 19 · 19 c · mit Rohrlehne

Sessel Nr. 19 I · 42 × 42 Cm · K 9.50
Sessel Nr. 19 I c · mit Rohrlehne · K 12.—

Halbfauteuil Nr. 19 I · 45 × 45 Cm · K 14.—
Halbfauteuil Nr. 19 I c · mit Rohrlehne · K 17.—

Sessel Nr. 20 · 42 Cm Durchm. · K 9.50

Fauteuil Nr. 20 · 52 Cm Durchm. · K 12.—

hiezu gehörig: Halbfauteuil Nr. 20½ · 45 × 45 Cm · K 10.50
Kanapee Nr. 20 · 135 Cm · K 35.—

Halbfauteuil Nr. 24½ · 48 × 51 Cm · K 16.—
hiezu gehörig: Sessel Nr. 24 · 45 × 45 Cm · K 13.—

Sessel Nr. 25 · 42 × 42 Cm · K 11.—

Halbfauteuil Nr. 25½ · 45 × 45 Cm · K 14.—

Sessel Nr. 22 · 45 × 45 Cm · K 20.—

Kanapee Nr. 22 · 150 Cm · K 80.—

Fauteuil Nr. 22 · 52 × 55 Cm · K 30.—

endless variety of curves. He combined the solid pieces with laminated sections, added seats of cane or wood, and came up with chairs that were light, strong, and inexpensive to produce.

Thonet's chairs had an elegant modern look that caught the eye of furniture buyers everywhere. By the end of the nineteenth century bentwood chairs from his factories could be found in Parisian cafés, middle-class English drawing rooms, Australian frontier settlements, and American parlors and restaurants.

While Thonet's chairs were reaching into more and more places, and mass-production techniques made chairs of all types available to greater numbers of people, the kings and queens of England and other countries still sat on thrones on ceremonial occasions. Thrones played an important role in the tribal life of nineteenth-century Africa also. However, most of the African thrones were not chairs but elaborately carved stools.

Opposite: Late nineteenth-century advertisement for bentwood chairs and a settee designed by Michael Thonet. The New York Public Library

*Wood stool with standing female
figure carved by the Buli master of
Zaire, late nineteenth century.* The
Metropolitan Museum of Art,
Purchase, Buckeye Trust and
Charles B. Berenson Gifts,
Rogers Fund, and funds from
various donors, 1979
(1979.290)

CHAPTER EIGHT

The Golden Stool of the Ashanti

At first glance, the polished wooden object doesn't look like a stool. Instead it appears to be a sculpture of an old woman, bent under the load she carries on her head. Her hands, twice as large as normal, emphasize how heavy it is. But then one takes a second look and realizes that the old woman's load is a seat, and the structure is a very special kind of stool.

Carved from a single block of wood more than a century ago, the stool is typical of those that were made for the rulers of central African kingdoms in what is today the Republic of Zaire. No one knows who designed and sculpted the stool, since African craftsmen did not sign their work. But because it was found near the town of Buli in southeastern Zaire, its creator is described as the "Buli master."

This stool, like others from central Africa, was actually a throne. Most Africans, young and old, sat or squatted on the ground or on mats in their dwellings. But the tribe's chief sat on a stool. It represented his power and authority, and each of its features had a symbolic meaning.

Most people in central Africa trace their ancestry through their mothers and grandmothers. That explains why the carved figure supporting the seat of a chief's stool was usually a woman. She stood for his female ancestors, and her braided hairstyle and intricately patterned body scars confirmed that she came from a wealthy, highborn family.

After Portuguese traders made contact with the central African kingdoms in the nineteenth century, some of the kingdoms' rulers ordered thrones modeled on European chairs. They had wooden backs and leather-covered seats. However, the rungs and splats of these new-type thrones featured decorations that were uniquely African. Rows of carved figures depicted everyday scenes of hunting, cooking, and eating alongside others that portrayed the tribe's initiation ceremonies. Together, the carvings offered a clear and lively picture of the society over which the chief presided.

Some of the most splendid African stools and thrones were found in those parts of the continent

BELOW: Wood chief's chair from Cameroon in West Africa. The rows of faces at the bottom represent the skulls of slain enemies, while the leopards carved on the arms are symbols of royal power. The chief rides the leopard at the left. The Cleveland Museum of Art, Gift in memory of his parents, Wheeler B. and Dorothy Preston, by Mary and John Preston, 83.33

African chief's chair from Angola with figures engaged in everyday activities carved on the back and the rungs. The Metropolitan Museum of Art, The Michael C. Rockefeller Memorial Collection, Purchase, Nelson A. Rockefeller Gift, 1970 (1978.412.619)

where gold was mined. Without doubt the most famous of all was the Golden Stool of the Ashanti people, who lived in West Africa.

In the Ashanti state of old, villages were grouped into territorial divisions. The chief of the largest village in each territory also ruled as the chief of the division. Every chief had his own ceremonial stool, made for him when he came to power and often covered with silver. After the chief's death, his stool would be blackened with soot and placed in the community's stool room along with those of all the chiefs who had preceded him. There it would remain forever as a memorial to the dead leader.

Ruling over the divisional chiefs was the king of the Ashanti, who resided in the national capital, Kumasi. Each new king was installed on the magnificent Golden Stool, and vowed to safeguard and preserve it throughout his reign.

A legend told how the great king Osei Tutu acquired the Golden Stool in the first place. According to the story, it was created by the magic of one of his priests. While the king looked on in amazement, the priest brought the stool down from the sky in a black cloud, amid rumblings and in air thick with white dust.

The wooden stool adorned with gold landed gently

at Osei Tutu's feet. The priest then announced that the stool contained the soul of the entire Ashanti nation, and he issued a solemn warning. If any harm came to the stool, the people would lose their courage and strength.

It's doubtful that the Golden Stool actually descended from the sky, but we do know that it dates to the time of Osei Tutu, who ruled the Ashanti nation at the beginning of the eighteenth century. We also know that it was venerated by the people and became the symbol of authority for all the Ashanti kings who followed him.

Unlike most Ashanti stools, which were rectangular in shape, the Golden Stool had a round seat and base. Much of it was covered with gold plate, and golden bells and the figurines of slain enemies hung from the rim of the seat. The king of the Ashanti sat on the

A chief's stool from Zaire, with a round seat and base like the Golden Stool of the Ashanti. The Metropolitan Museum of Art, The Michael C. Rockefeller Memorial Collection, Purchase, Nelson A. Rockefeller Gift, 1969 (1978.412.593)

stool only when he was installed and once each year thereafter. On great public occasions, the stool was displayed on a special stand of its own, since the Ashanti believed it must never again touch the ground.

Nothing happened to disrupt the rule of the Ashanti kings or endanger the Golden Stool until a British military force invaded the nation in 1874. The British defeated the Ashanti and organized the coastal region as the colony of the Gold Coast. But the Ashanti remained in power in the interior. Prempeh was installed as king in 1894, and two years later he led his people in fresh attacks against the British occupiers.

The British arrested Prempeh and exiled him to the Seychelles Islands, far away off the east coast of Africa. They did not gain custody of the Golden Stool, however. After Prempeh's arrest, the stool's guardians removed it by night from the capital, Kumasi, and transported it to a remote village, where they hid it carefully.

The British governor, Sir Frederic Hodgson, was determined to possess the stool. As long as it remained in Ashanti hands, he feared it might be used to install another king. He met in Kumasi with Ashanti leaders and said: "I am the representative of the queen of England, who now rules this country. Where is the Golden

Stool? I should be sitting on it, not this chair."

The leaders were offended by the governor's words and refused to reveal the stool's location. Then he heard a rumor that it was hidden near the village of Bari. Acting quickly, Hodgson sent a squad of soldiers to the village with orders to find the stool and bring it back at once to Kumasi.

When the soldiers got to the village, they saw only children in the streets. They asked them where all the grown-ups were, and the children replied that their fathers had gone out hunting and their mothers were working in the vegetable gardens. Then the soldiers asked the youngsters where the Golden Stool was hidden, and threatened to punish them if they didn't tell. When the children said nothing, the soldiers grabbed several of the bigger boys and began to beat them.

One child managed to sneak away

Seated chief with lance. Carving from Mali, in West Africa, late nineteenth–early twentieth century. The Metropolitan Museum of Art, Gift of Kronos Collections in honor of Martin Lerner, 1983 (1983.600)

and tell the grown-ups what was happening. Furious, they hurried back to the village and confronted the soldiers. In the fighting that followed, shots were fired and two of the soldiers were wounded. The rest fled in the direction of Kumasi while the villagers chanted:

Instead of the stool the governor shall have
the white men's heads sent to him in Kumasi.
The Golden Stool shall be well washed in
the white men's blood.

News of the incident spread rapidly throughout the kingdom, and the Ashanti rose in revolt. From April to July 1900, they besieged the fort in Kumasi where Governor Hodgson had taken refuge. At last the governor succeeded in escaping, but he left for England shortly thereafter and never returned.

In September 1900, the British finally put down the revolt, and the following year they made the entire Ashanti kingdom part of the colony of the Gold Coast. A new British governor, Sir Matthew Nathan, arrived and said he would not interfere with the religion and customs of the Ashanti. He also said he had no interest in the Golden Stool. But the Ashanti leaders obviously did not trust Nathan, for the stool remained in its secret hiding place.

A young Ashanti chief poses with his advisers and members of his family in this photograph taken about 1910. The large umbrella is a symbol of the chief's position. The Bettmann Archive

In 1920, yet another British governor, Sir Gordon Guggisberg, took charge of the Gold Coast colony. He announced that the aging Prempeh, who had been in exile now for twenty-four years, would be permitted to return to his country if one condition was met. The Ashanti must turn over the Golden Stool to the British.

Before any decision was reached, the whereabouts of the stool came to light in a different and startling way. In 1921 some of the stool's golden ornaments turned up for sale in a market near Kumasi. The local chiefs traced the sellers and discovered that they included the men responsible for the stool's safekeeping. They had stripped the wooden stool of almost all its precious ornamentation.

When the Ashanti heard what the men had done, they went into mourning for their beloved Golden Stool. The chiefs' council brought the accused to trial and sentenced six of them to death, saying they had "betrayed the country and opened it to disgrace and ridicule."

The British superior court refused to confirm the sentence, feeling it was too harsh, and the convicted men were deported for life instead. But the governor wisely said that the British had no claim on what was left of the Golden Stool. The Ashanti repaired and restored it, incorporating as many of the original ornaments as possible.

In 1924, Prempeh returned at last from exile as a private citizen. After promising that he would not attempt to regain his former position as king, he was given the Golden Stool to keep. He never sat on it, however. When Prempeh died in 1931, the stool was put on display for all his mourners to see and admire. But no one was permitted to photograph it.

Today the Ashanti nation is part of the West African country of Ghana, which won its independence from Great Britain in 1957. The Golden Stool is preserved as a sacred relic in the city of Kumasi, and remains a potent symbol of Ashanti strength, unity, and pride.

Back at the beginning of the twentieth century, when the British governor was trying to seize the Golden Stool, European and American explorers and traders were bringing home examples of African stools, sculptures, masks, and other objects. Exhibited in museums, these works had a tremendous influence on European and American artists such as Pablo Picasso, Constantin Brancusi, and Frank Lloyd Wright. And many of the same artists tried their hands at designs for furniture, especially designs for chairs.

Dining table and eight side chairs designed by Frank Lloyd Wright for the Joseph M. Husser house in Chicago, 1899. The Domino's Center for Architecture and Design

CHAPTER NINE

"A Machine for Sitting In"

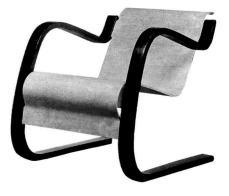

Frank Lloyd Wright, one of the greatest American architects of the twentieth century, believed that houses were like living things, and that every part should relate to every other part. That included the furniture.

"The most truly satisfactory houses," Wright wrote in 1908, "are those in which most or all of the furniture is built as part of the original scheme. The whole must always be considered as an integral unit."

Influenced by the low, horizontal lines of Japanese buildings, Wright designed houses in the American midwest that differed sharply from the elaborate dwellings that were fashionable at the time. Instead of steeply gabled roofs, turrets, and wraparound porches, Wright's houses had flat roofs and a simple, direct appearance based on rectangles and squares rather than curves.

It was hard to find furniture that suited Wright's houses. As he himself said, "All available is senselessly ornate." So Wright began to design his own cabinets, tables, and chairs in the same spare style that characterized his architecture.

One of his earliest and most famous chair designs was for a tall, straight side chair with a slatted back. When four or more of the chairs were placed around a dining table, their backs served as screens that defined the eating area and helped to create a room within a room.

Some critics have charged that the chairs' rigid, upright backs make them uncomfortable. But in Wright's day, when most women still wore corsets and everyone took pains to sit up straight at table, the chairs seemed perfectly acceptable.

The houses, office buildings, and other structures that Wright and his contemporaries designed would not have been possible without the technological advances that occurred one after another in the early years of the twentieth century. Before 1890, few American or European homes had central heating, indoor plumbing, hot and cold running water, or electric light and power. Virtually no office or apartment buildings were equipped with elevators. By 1920, all of the new technologies had become commonplace.

At first these developments had little effect on chair design, since people still sat the same way they always had. But social shifts after World War I brought about many changes in furniture design.

People moved more often and tended to live in smaller houses and apartments, which required less in the way of furnishings. Domestic help was harder to get and more costly than it had been before the war. Consequently, people sought chairs and other furniture pieces that could be maintained with as little effort as possible. Above all, a wave of experimentation swept through all the arts and crafts in the first postwar years.

One of the boldest innovators in chair design was a Dutchman, Gerrit Rietveld. The son of a cabinetmaker, Rietveld left school at eleven to work as an apprentice in his father's shop. At the age of twelve he made a set of chairs and a table of sticks and boards that survive in Holland today.

In 1919 Rietveld joined the Dutch design group known as "De Stijl" ("The Style"). Its members, who included the painter Piet Mondrian, believed that

The Red and Blue Chair, designed in 1919 by Gerrit Rietveld. Private collection, New York. Photo courtesy Barry Friedman Ltd.

through total simplification and abstraction they could achieve a universal harmony in their work. For Rietveld, this meant making chairs composed of horizontal and vertical planes, some of which he painted in the three primary colors, red, yellow, and blue.

Looking like abstract paintings in three dimensions, Rietveld's chairs created a striking impression when they were put on display. Their hard surfaces and sharp edges made them uncomfortable to sit on, however. As a result they proved to be of greater interest to museum curators than to private customers.

Rietveld's chairs also interested other designers of modern furniture, who incorporated some of his ideas in their own work. Among the most prominent of these were two young European architects, Marcel Breuer and Ludwig Mies van der Rohe.

Breuer and Mies van der Rohe both taught at the Bauhaus, a German design school that attempted to unite art and commerce. Whether they were planning a house, a chair, or a dish, the Bauhaus artists eliminated all unnecessary decoration and emphasized the basic geometrical shape of the object. They made sketches, samples, and full-scale models that, they hoped, would be bought by manufacturers and put into mass production.

Inspired by the curved metal handlebars on his bicycle, Marcel Breuer in the mid-1920s constructed a new type of armchair from chrome steel tubing. One continuous piece of bent tubular steel formed the basic frame of the chair, which had no legs as such. Other tubular pieces were used for the back, the seat, and as braces below the arms. Fabric panels instead of upholstery stretched across the seat and back, and provided armrests.

Armchair of tubular steel and fabric designed by Marcel Breuer about 1925. The Metropolitan Museum of Art, Purchase, Theodore R. Gamble, Jr., Gift, in honor of his mother, Mrs. Theodore Robert Gamble, 1985 (1985.256)

Later, in 1928, Breuer created an even more unusual metal chair. It was cantilevered, which meant that it was supported at one end only. Other designers had experimented with similar chairs, but Breuer claimed he had gotten the idea on his own by turning a tubular steel stool on its side, placing a seat on top, and adding a back.

Breuer's cantilevered side chair consisted of a single piece of continuously curved metal tubing and two pieces of canvas, one stretched across the seat, the other across the back. It eliminated costly joints, as well as complicated construction and upholstery, and served as the model for many other side chairs.

Ludwig Mies van der Rohe, Breuer's colleague at the Bauhaus, designed a more elaborate type of metal chair. Because Mies made it for the German pavilion at a 1929 exhibition in Barcelona, Spain, it was called the "Barcelona chair." The chair had an elegant simplicity. Two curved metal bars bent down to support the seat while two others rose in the opposite direction to form the back. Straps across both the seat and the back provided a base for matching leather-covered cushions.

"A house is a machine for living in . . . an armchair is a machine for sitting in," the twentieth-century French architect and designer Le Corbusier had proclaimed. And many of the metal chairs designed by Mies, Breuer, and others did, in fact, resemble machines. As such they were perfectly suited to the stark, uncluttered interiors of modern glass-and-steel buildings.

The chairs did not please everyone, however. Their critics complained that they weren't much more comfortable to sit in than Rietveld's chairs. A well-designed easy chair, they said, should permit the sitter to turn from one side to the other and lean forward or back.

The Barcelona chair designed by Ludwig Mies van der Rohe for Knoll. Photo courtesy The Knoll Group

Otherwise, the body's muscles and joints would tend to stiffen. But in Breuer's and Mies's chairs, the sitter usually had to remain in one position. The seats and backs offered little if anything in the way of cushioning, and the lack of arms on many of the chairs made getting up from them difficult.

Metal chairs might be fine for factories, hospitals, office buildings, and hotel lobbies, the critics concluded, but would you really want them in your living room?

Except for wealthy trendsetters, most people of the time seemed to agree with the critics. They might purchase inexpensive copies of Breuer's side chairs for their kitchens or bathrooms. But after working all day at machines, the last thing they wanted was to come home to a house or apartment furnished entirely with machinelike metal chairs.

Far more pleasing to the average man and woman were the modern wooden chairs that the Finnish architect and designer Alvar Aalto began to make in the late 1920s. Their grainy surfaces had an inviting warmth that no metal chair could match.

Aalto applied principles developed by Michael Thonet a century earlier to bend the laminated wooden frames for his cantilevered chairs. For the one-piece seat he used a material that had only recently been perfected—plywood. Like a laminate, plywood consisted of thin layers of wood that were glued together under pressure to form a solid board. But in plywood the grain of each layer was placed at right angles to the grain of the next instead of running in the opposite direction.

Before World War I, plywood had been used mainly as a cheap substitute for wood in such things as

Cantilevered armchair designed by Alvar Aalto about 1930–1933. The chair's arms and supports are of painted bentwood, while the seat and back are made of birch plywood. The Metropolitan Museum of Art, Purchase, Robert and Meryl Gift, 1984 (1984.223)

packing crates, or on the backs of bureaus where it would not be seen. During the war, with wood in short supply, it was employed in the construction of boats and airplanes and proved to have certain advantages over natural boards. Unlike them, plywood had no tendency to split or warp, and it could be shaped easily for use in chairs like Aalto's. It was also inexpensive — an important consideration for furniture manufacturers and customers in the Depression years of the 1930s.

A husband-and-wife designer team, Charles and Ray Eames, developed a unique plywood chair as a result of an assignment they were given during World War II. The Navy commissioned the Eameses to create a lightweight leg splint that would fit comfortably and snugly around an injured leg. After solving the problem with molded plywood, the Eameses decided to try making a plywood armchair that, like the splint, would be contoured to fit the human body.

The Eameses united the seat, back, and arms of the chair in a single form shaped over a cast-iron mold. They covered this form with a layer of foam rubber—which had begun to be used in chairs instead of springs—and cemented the upholstery fabric on top of it. Then they added legs of aluminum or wood.

The chair caught on quickly, and the Eameses designed many variations of it. Some models had arms, some did not. Some were upholstered, others left the plywood surface exposed.

In the late 1940s the Eameses began to make similar molded chairs out of glass-fiber-reinforced plastic. These chairs, with their body-fitting curves and pleasing colors, possessed great strength and durability. They could be mounted on all sorts of legs and bases, and used in a variety of settings. Within a few years, inexpensive copies of the Eameses' original designs could be found in homes and offices all over the world.

Other designers, like the renowned Finnish-American architect Eero Saarinen, took the Eameses' ideas a step further. Saarinen covered the plastic shells of his armchairs with thick wool upholstery. Then he mounted the shells on four slender metal legs or, later, a

An assortment of molded fiberglass chairs designed by Charles and Ray Eames. The molded fiberglass process was introduced commercially in 1950, and most of these chairs are still being manufactured. Photo courtesy Herman Miller Inc.

A chimney sweep naps in Eero Saarinen's "Womb chair," so called because it seemed to surround and protect the sitter. Advertising photo from the Knoll Archives, courtesy The Knoll Group

single pedestal that widened out into a circular base.

"A chair should look well as a piece of sculpture in a room," Saarinen once wrote. "It should also look well when someone is sitting in it. And finally it should be flattering to the person sitting in it."

While manufacturers were putting chairs like the Eameses' and Saarinen's into mass production, craftsmen were creating unusual easy chairs for a small luxury market. There was the plastic "Blow" chair of the 1960s that could be inflated or deflated as the sitter desired. There was also the Sacco, an Italian chair that operated on the principle of the beanbag. It consisted of a leather sack filled with plastic granules that shifted around whenever the sitter changed position.

Most of these experimental easy chairs proved to be more eye-catching than practical. Then, in the 1970s and 1980s, a totally different kind of chair appeared on the scene. Like the thrones and state chairs of the past, it was more than just a seat. But unlike them, it was not really meant for sitting at all.

CHAPTER TEN

A Perfect Chair?

One object looks like a big toy automobile. It has a bumper, a front grille, two working headlights, floppy fenders, and a windshield. And it rests on wheels.

Another object is the exact image of a sitting Mickey Mouse. Its legs are bent, its arms outstretched, its smiling face is turned to one side, and its tail props up the creature in the back.

Although it would be hard to guess, both objects are actually armchairs. Both of them can be sat upon, too — although that obviously isn't their primary purpose.

These "chairs" represent a trend in recent years toward making seats that are really sculptures. Museums exhibit them as examples of the latest in modern art, and individuals purchase them for their private collections. They may even sit on them occasionally, but the chairs are usually too valuable for that.

Some contemporary chairs are meant to be appreciated both as sculptures and as seats. In the 1970s and 1980s, the young sculptor Scott Burton shaped granite stools, benches, and chairs for parks and other public places in many American cities. Some of his rough

An armchair designed by Gary Schatmeyer in the form of an auto uses shiny fabric for the bumper and grille. The headrest is shaped like a windshield, complete with rearview mirror. New York Times Pictures

stone seats made viewers think of prehistoric thrones. They and his more polished chairs and stools reflected Burton's belief that art should "place itself not just in front of, but around, behind, and underneath (literally) the audience."

Mickey Mouse chair designed by Catherine Walsh. New York Times Pictures

However, Burton's stone furniture has serious limitations. Since the pieces each weigh between eight hundred and three thousand pounds, they cannot be moved easily and usually stay wherever they are first set down. Also, their hard surfaces and sharp edges discourage sitters from remaining on them for more than a few minutes.

The late Scott Burton in 1986, with the granite tables and stools he designed for a plaza in New York City. New York Times Pictures

While Burton and others have been treating chairs as art objects, contemporary craftsmen have been trying to design chairs that will do a better job of accommodating the human body. Their goal: to create the perfect chair.

One of the best-known and most successful of these craftsmen is Peter Danko, who has a workshop in Maryland. His Bodyform chair takes Michael Thonet's nineteenth-century bentwood techniques to a new, high-tech extreme. A big press comes down and molds the chair—legs, seat, and back—from a single piece of plywood.

When Danko was developing the mold for the Body-form chair, he pulled people in off the street and had them sit down on the trial shapes he had made from laminated wood. He tested and discarded more than twenty different varia-tions of the chair before settling on one that met his standards for comfort.

Danko is also very con-cerned about the strength and durability of his furni-ture. "A chair can't weigh more than fifteen pounds," he once said, "but it has to be able to support more than two-hundred-and-fifty pounds. And it has to be able to withstand some-body leaning on the back legs, going sideways, or

The Bodyform chair designed by Peter Danko. Photo courtesy Peter Danko & Associates, Inc.

running the chair across thick carpet when they push off."

When Danko was designing his Waveform chair, which was a bentwood frame and upholstered seat and back cushions, he became concerned about its durability. He wanted the chair to flex in several different ways, but he didn't want it to be "too resilient, or else the sitter would feel that the chair was unstable." So he devised a unique means of testing it.

First the designer piled 180 pounds of lead bullets on the chair's seat. Then he attached a special machine he had made to the frame. Switched on, the machine

Two of Peter Danko's Waveform chairs. Photo courtesy Peter Danko & Associates, Inc.

rocked and twisted the chair more than 50,000 times. Only after it held up under this test—"a beating beyond that any chair would normally undergo," according to Danko—did the designer put the Waveform chair into production.

Although Peter Danko's chairs are his own original creations, they don't differ sharply in appearance from some of the classic chairs of the past. But one modern chair designed to encourage healthier sitting looks like no other chair of past or present. It is the "Balans" chair, made in Norway and distributed in many other countries including the United States.

Instead of being flat or slanting back, the seat of the "Balans" chair tilts forward. The chair has no backrest because one is not needed, but it does have a knee rest so that the sitter won't slide off the seat.

Health experts say that the "Balans" chair is built on the ergonomic principle, which means that it has been shaped to fit the specific needs of the body. One half sits, half kneels in a "Balans" chair, and after an initial feeling of strangeness the experience is surprisingly pleasant.

The forward-slanting seat and supportive leg cushion lead automatically to a straightening of the spine. This reduces the likelihood of lower-back pain, which often strikes when one curves the spine to lean forward in a conventional chair. Sitting on a "Balans" chair also lessens the strain on the neck and shoulders, especially when one works for long periods at a desk or keyboard.

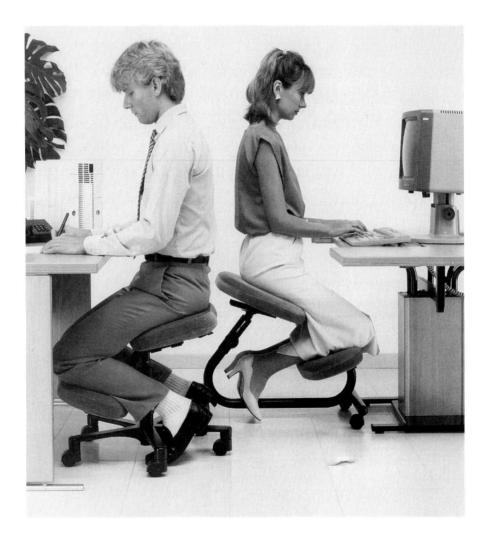

A young man and woman at work in "Balans" chairs. Photo courtesy Håg, Inc.

While the "Balans" chair and other experimental models have many supporters, most people still prefer the more traditional styles. Antique European and American chairs command high prices at auctions and in antique shops. Less expensive but well-made reproductions are available in furniture stores everywhere.

Many stores and catalogues feature the "early-American look" in copies of Windsor chairs, rockers, Shaker chairs, and wing chairs (but without chamber pots in the seats). The overstuffed easy chairs of the Victorian era, upholstered in floral patterns and covered with pillows, are enjoying a new popularity also.

Since World War II travel time has shrunk dramatically, and an international culture has come into being. As a result, chairs can now be found in many places around the world where they once were rare. In their homes, Japanese people may still kneel on floor mats and Arabs may sit cross-legged on beautiful rugs. But if you checked into a hotel in Tokyo or Damascus, you'd find chairs in your room. And if you attended a meeting or went to a restaurant in one of those cities, chances are you wouldn't be expected to sit on the floor.

Today there are few historical boundaries, either, as far as chairs are concerned. A typical middle-class home contains chairs from many different periods. In the living room, there may be a pair of eighteenth-century wing chairs, a bentwood rocker, and a clean-lined modern easy chair. In the kitchen, metal chairs adapted from Marcel Breuer's cantilevered models may surround the table.

This sort of mix will probably continue in the future. No one type of chair, antique or modern, upholstered or plain, is ever likely to satisfy everyone's ideas of style and comfort. Just as it takes all kinds of people to form a community or a country, so it takes all kinds of chairs to furnish an inviting home.

While few of today's chairs indicate a person's power or rank, they still have meanings beyond their function as seats. Like the chairs of the past, they reveal many things about their owners — their tastes, their values, their economic status.

Chairs also reflect, as they always have, the customs and habits of the societies in which they are used. Just as seat furniture tells us much about life in ancient Egypt or medieval Europe, so your favorite chair conveys a great deal about you, and the time in which you live.

Bibliography and
Source Notes

Many different books and articles provided the information found in this book. The listing of sources that follows is organized by chapter, and in sequence within each chapter. As a result, it can be used to pursue a topic that the reader wishes to explore further. Those books that were written for young people are indicated with asterisks.

Overall

The idea for the book came from "Comfortably Seated," an exhibit of antique and modern chairs that I saw at The Cleveland Museum of Art in 1986. The range and variety of chairs on display fascinated me, and the exhibition brochure gave me a preliminary list of topics to investigate.

Four histories of furniture were especially helpful, and were referred to for almost every chapter. The books and their authors are:

Gloag, John. *A Social History of Furniture Design, from B.C. 1300 to A.D. 1960.* London: Cassell, 1966; New York: Crown, 1966.

Hayward, Helena, editor. *World Furniture.* New York and Toronto: McGraw-Hill, 1965.

Lucie-Smith, Edward. *Furniture: A Concise History.* London: Thames and Hudson, 1979.

Wheeler, James, et al. Introduction by Sir Francis Watson. *The History of Furniture.* New York: Morrow, 1976.

Two other books offered valuable insights into the use and meaning of chairs in various cultures and periods. These were:

Gloag, John. *The Chair: Its Origins, Designs, and Social History.* South Brunswick, New Jersey, and New York: A. S. Barnes, 1967. (This book focuses on English chairs, and was published in England under the title *The Englishman's Chair.*)

Rybczynski, Witold. *Home: A Short History of an Idea.* New York: Viking, 1986.

Rybczynski, Witold. *Home: A Short History of an Idea.* New York: Viking, 1986. (Discusses chairs and other furniture in relation to changing notions of domestic comfort from the Middle Ages to the present. Although the book was written for adults, its lively style can be enjoyed by younger readers.)

Chapter One

Advantages of kneeling and squatting
Rudofsky, Bernard. *Now I Lay Me Down to Eat.* Garden City, New York: Anchor Press/Doubleday, 1980.
Rybczynski, *Home*

Seating customs in the Middle East
Hayward, *World Furniture*

Seating customs in Japan
Hayward, *World Furniture*
Morse, Edward S. *Japanese Homes and Their Surroundings.* New York: Dover, 1961.

Prehistoric stools, chairs, and thrones
Gloag, *The Chair*

Description of King Solomon's Throne
The Holy Bible, Authorized King James Version. Iowa Falls, Iowa: World Bible Publishers.

Chapter Two

Stools and chairs in ancient Egypt
Gloag, *The Chair*
————, *A Social History of Furniture Design*
Hawley, Henry H. *Comfortably Seated* (exhibition brochure). Cleveland: The Cleveland Museum of Art, 1986.
Hayward, *World Furniture*
*Stead, Miriam. *Egyptian Life.* Cambridge, Massachusetts: Harvard University Press, 1986.

Description and photographs of King Tutankhamen's throne
Riesterer, Peter P. *Egyptian Museum Cairo.* Berne, Switzerland: Kümmerly & Frey, 1968.

Ancient Greek chairs
Gloag, *A Social History of Furniture Design*
Hayward, *World Furniture*
*Jenkins, Ian. *Greek and Roman Life.* Cambridge, Massachusetts: Harvard University Press, 1986.

Lucie-Smith, *Furniture*

Chairs in ancient Rome
Gloag, *A Social History of Furniture Design*
Hayward, *World Furniture*
Jenkins, *Greek and Roman Life*
Lucie-Smith, *Furniture*
Wheeler, *The History of Furniture*

Chapter Three

Misericords
Laird, Marshall. *English Misericords*. London: John Murray, 1986.
Lucie-Smith, *Furniture*

Peasants' seat furniture
Hayward, *World Furniture*

Furniture of medieval merchants and craftsmen
Rybczynski, *Home*

Chairs and other seats in castles
Lucie-Smith, *Furniture*

Great Britain's coronation chair
Gloag, *The Chair*

Furniture in Renaissance Holland
Rybczynski, *Home*

Backstools and armchairs
Gloag, *The Chair*
Hayward, *World Furniture*

Early upholstered chairs and quotation from Sir John Harington
Beard, Geoffrey. *The National Trust Book of English Furniture*. New York: Viking Penguin, 1985.

Chapter Four

Chairs in India and quotation from Sir Dudley North
Lucie-Smith, *Furniture*

Chinese chairs and stools
Hayward, *World Furniture*
Kates, George N. *Chinese Household Furniture*. New York: Dover, 1948.

Chapter Five

Life at Versailles
Lewis, W. H. *The Splendid Century: Life in the France of Louis XIV*. New York: Morrow, 1954.
Lucie-Smith, *Furniture*
Rybczynski, *Home*
Wheeler, *The History of Furniture*

Baroque furniture and the "Canopy of State"
Wheeler, *The History of Furniture*

Upholstered chairs in the 1700s
Beard, *The National Trust Book of English Furniture*
Gloag, *The Chair*
Rybczynski, *Home*

Chapter Six

Children's chairs
Beard, *The National Trust Book of English Furniture*

Roles of different craftsmen in the making of chairs
Hayward, *World Furniture*

Thomas Chippendale's chairs
Gloag, *The Chair*
Hayward, *World Furniture*

The standard parts of a chair
Beard, *The National Trust Book of English Furniture*

George Hepplewhite's chairs
Hayward, *World Furniture*

Quotation from Hepplewhite
Beard, *The National Trust Book of English Furniture*

Thomas Sheraton and his chair designs
Gloag, *The Chair*
Hayward, *World Furniture*

The neoclassical style in chairs
Wheeler, *The History of Furniture*

Anecdote about King George III and the Windsor chair
Gloag, *The Chair*

Windsor chairs in general
Gloag, *A Social History of Furniture Design*
Hayward, *World Furniture*

The easy chair
Heckscher, Morrison H. *In Quest of Comfort: The Easy Chair in America.* New York: The Metropolitan Museum of Art, 1971.

Chairmaking in Colonial America
Wheeler, *The History of Furniture*

The rocking chair
Gloag, *The Chair*
Lucie-Smith, *Furniture*

Chapter Seven

Shaker chairs
Lucie-Smith, *Furniture*
McFadden, David Revere. *Furniture in the Collection of the Cooper-Hewitt Museum.* New York: The Smithsonian Institution, 1979.
Sprigg, June. *Shaker Design.* New York: The Whitney Museum of American Art in association with W. W. Norton & Co., 1986.

Additional information on the Shakers
Harris, William H., and Judith S. Levey, editors. *The New Columbia Encyclopedia.* New York and London: Columbia University Press, 1975.

Empire chair styles in France
Lucie-Smith, *Furniture*

Duncan Phyfe's Federal designs
Hayward, *World Furniture*
Wheeler, *The History of Furniture*

Bath chairs
Gloag, *The Chair*

Wheelchairs
Kamenetz, Herman L., M.D. *The Wheelchair Book.* Springfield, Illinois: Charles C Thomas, 1969.

Overstuffed chairs
Hayward, *World Furniture*
Lucie-Smith, *Furniture*

Gloag, *The Chair*

Michael Thonet and his bentwood chairs
Hayward, *World Furniture*
Lucie-Smith, *Furniture*
McFadden, *Furniture in the Collection of the Cooper-Hewitt Museum*
Ostergard, Derek E., editor. *Bent Wood and Metal Furniture: 1850–1946*. New York: The American Federation of Arts, 1987.
Wheeler, *The History of Furniture*

Chapter Eight
The Buli master's stool
Wall label, "Art of Africa" display, The Metropolitan Museum of Art

Stools and chairs in Central Africa
Gillon, Werner. *A Short History of African Art*. New York: Penguin, 1986.
Wall labels, "Art of Africa" display, The Metropolitan Museum of Art

Stools of the Ashanti chiefs
Gillon, *A Short History of African Art*

Appearance of the Golden Stool
Balmer, the Rev. W. T. *A History of the Akan Peoples of the Gold Coast*. New York: Negro Universities Press, 1969.
Flynn, J. K. *Asante and Its Neighbors, 1700–1807*. London: Longmans, 1971.
*———. *A Junior History of Ghana*. London: Longmans, 1975.

Exile of King Prempeh and British attempts to seize the Golden Stool
Balmer, *A History of the Akan Peoples*
Kimble, David. *A Political History of Ghana*. Oxford: The Clarendon Press, 1963.
Lewin, Thomas J. *Asante Before the British: The Prempean Years, 1875–1900*. Lawrence, Kansas: The Regents Press of Kansas, 1978.

Quotation from Sir Frederic Hodgson and chant of the Ashanti villagers
Kimble, *A Political History of Ghana*

The Ashanti revolt, its aftermath, and the discovery of the Golden Stool
Bourret, F. M. *Ghana, the Road to Independence, 1919–1957*. Stanford, California: Stanford University Press, 1949, 1960.
Kimble, *A Political History of Ghana*
Tordoff, William. *Ashanti Under the Prempehs, 1888–1935*. London: Oxford University Press, 1965.

Return of Prempeh
Kimble, *A Political History of Ghana*
Tordoff, *Ashanti Under the Prempehs*

The Golden Stool in an independent Ghana
Lystad, Robert A. *The Ashanti: A Proud People.* New York: Greenwood, 1968.
　　Helpful information about the Golden Stool and Ghana was also provided by Mr. Horace Anguah-Dei, Assistant Information Officer at the Embassy of Ghana in Washington, D.C.

Chapter Nine
Frank Lloyd Wright's chair designs
Hanks, David A. *The Decorative Designs of Frank Lloyd Wright.* New York: Dutton, 1979.
Lucie-Smith, *Furniture*
Wheeler, *The History of Furniture*

Technological advances and social changes in the early twentieth century
Rybczynski, *Home*
Wheeler, *The History of Furniture*

Gerrit Rietveld and his chairs
Hayward, *World Furniture*
Lucie-Smith, *Furniture*
Reif, Rita. "Chairs That Suggest Mondrians Come to Life." Article in *The New York Times*, October 2, 1988.
Wheeler, *The History of Furniture*

Marcel Breuer's chair designs
Hayward, *World Furniture*
Lucie-Smith, *Furniture*
Ostergard, *Bent Wood and Metal Furniture*
Wheeler, *The History of Furniture*

Ludwig Mies van der Rohe and the "Barcelona chair"
Hayward, *World Furniture*
Johnson, Philip. *Mies van der Rohe.* New York: The Museum of Modern Art, 1978.

Quotation from Le Corbusier
Jeanneret, Charles-Edouard (Le Corbusier). *Towards a New Architecture,* translated by Frederick Etchells. London, John Rodker, 1931.

Discomforts of modern chairs
Rybczynski, *Home*

Chairs of Alvar Aalto and advances in plywood
Lucie-Smith, *Furniture*
Ostergard, *Bent Wood and Metal Furniture*

Charles and Ray Eames' chair designs
Drexler, Arthur. *Charles Eames: Furniture from the Design Collection.* New York: The
    Museum of Modern Art, 1973.
Hayward, *World Furniture*
Ostergard, *Bent Wood and Metal Furniture*
Wheeler, *The History of Furniture*

Eero Saarinen's chairs
Hayward, *World Furniture*
Wheeler, *The History of Furniture*

Quotation from Saarinen
    Biographical material on the designer provided by The Knoll Group, manufac-
turer of his chairs

Experimental easy chairs of the 1960s
Lucie-Smith, *Furniture*

Chapter Ten

Automobile and Mickey Mouse chairs
Giovannini, Joseph. "Chairs That Roar." Article in *The New York Times*, March 19,
    1987.

Scott Burton's stone furniture
Richardson, Brenda. *Scott Burton.* Baltimore: The Baltimore Museum of Art, 1986.
Smith, Roberta. Obituary of Scott Burton, *The New York Times*, January 1, 1990.

Peter Danko's chairs
Goodman, Susan. "Chairs With Souls for the Computer Age." Article in *The New
    York Times*, March 31, 1988.
Krasnow, Iris. "Chairman of the Board." Article in *Museum and Arts Washington*
    magazine, March/April 1989.

The "Balans" chair
Hawley, *Comfortably Seated*
Mandal, A. C. *The Seated Man.* Denmark: Dafnia Publications, 1985.
    Promotional material from Håg, Inc., distributors of the "Balans" chair

Index

Page numbers in italics refer to illustrations.

Aalto, Alvar, 107–8, *108*
Africa
    Ashanti people, 90–97, *95*
    Buli master, *86*, 87
    chief's chair, 88, *89*
    Golden Stool of the Ashanti, 90–97
    stool thrones, 85, *86*, 87–88, 90, *91*
America
    colonial period, *61*, 62–63, 64, *64*, 65, *65*, 66–70, *67*, *68*, *69*
    "early American look," 121
    Federal style, 76–77, *76*
    rocking chair, 66–70, *68*, *69*, 121
    Shaker style, *72*, 74–75, *75*, 121
    wheelchair first used in, 77, *80*
    Windsor chairs, 64, *64*, *65*, 121
    wing chairs, 65–66, *67*, 121
animals, for ornamentation
    feet, practice of using on legs, 15, *16*, 17, 18, *76*
    heads of, 11, 17
Arab peoples, furnishings of, 1–2, *2*, 121
armchairs
    ancient, 5
    bentwood, 83, *84*, 85
    Breuer, *104*
    cantilevered, 107–8, *108*
    Egyptian, 14
    French (baroque), 50–51, *50*, 53, *54*
    "French chairs," 56
    origin of name, 36, 38
    Renaissance, *35*, 36–38, *37*
    Roman, *23*, 24
    "running chairs," 53–54, *54*
    Shaker, *75*
    Waveform, 118–19, *118*
arrangement of seated furniture

in China, 42–43
in France, 51, 53
automobile chair (Schatmeyer), 113, *114*

backstools, 35–36
"Balans" chair, 119–21, *120*
Barcelona chair (Mies), 105–6, *106*
baroque style, 50–51, *50*, 53, *54*
Bath chairs, 77, *79*
Bauhaus style, 103–6, *104*, *106*
beanbag chair, 112
beds, as seats in Middle Ages, 29
benches
    built-in for dining, Middle Ages, 33
    dining, for monks, 26
    in Renaissance, 35
bentwood chairs, 83, *84*, 85
"Blow" chair, 112
Bodyform chair, 116–17, *117*
bow, 63
Brancusi, Constantin, 97
Breuer, Marcel, 103–5, *104*, 122
Buddha, 5, *6*
Buli master, *86*, 87
Burton, Scott, 114–16, *116*

Cabinet-Maker and Upholsterer's Drawing Book (Sheraton), 61–62
Cabinet-Maker and Upholsterer's Guide, The (Hepplewhite), 60–61, 62
cabinetmaking shops, 57–62
caning of chairs, 39–40, 42, 51, 70
canopy
    chairs with, 33
    French "Canopy of State," 51–52
cantilevered chairs, 104–5, 107–8, *108*, 122
carver, 57
"chair for an officer," 76
chair, history of
    in Africa, 85, *86*, 87–88, *89*, 90–97, *91*, *93*
    in America, *64*, 65, *65*, 66–70, *67*, *68*, *69*, 76–77, *76*
    in China, 42–43, *44–45*, 46

during Dark Ages, 25–27, *26*
in Egypt, 3, 10–11, *12, 13,* 14–15, *16,* 17
in England, 57–66, *60, 61, 62*
evolution from thrones, 5–6, 33
in France, 47–52, *49, 50, 52*–56, *54, 55,*
    75–76
in Greece, 17–21, *18, 20, 21*
in India, 39–40
"as machine for sitting in," 105
in Middle Ages, 27–34, *28, 30, 31, 34*
nineteenth-century, 77–85, *78, 79, 80, 81,*
    84
in Renaissance, 35–38, *35, 36, 37*
in Rome, 22–24, *22, 23*
Shaker, 74–75, *75*
twentieth century, *98,* 99–112, *102, 104,*
    106, 108, 110, 111, 113–22, *114, 115,*
    116, 117, 118, 120
upholstery introduced, *37,* 38
word "chair" enters English language,
    29
See also specific countries, specific furniture-
    makers, and specific styles of chairs
chair, parts of, 58–59, *58*
chairman, origin of term, 30
chamber pots, and seated furniture, 66
children's chairs, 57
China
    arrangement of chairs in, 42–43
    "barbarian couches" (early Chinese
        word for chair), 41
    chairs introduced to, 40–41
    coverings of chairs, 42
    curved-back chairs, *41,* 46
    customs and chairs, 42
    floors in, 43
    footrest built into chairs, 43, *44*
    furnishings of common people, 41–42
    furnishings of wealthy people, 41,
        42–43, *44, 45,* 46
    k'angs (sleeping platforms), 40, 42
    men, status of, and chairs, 42, *45*
    mortise and tenon construction in, 43
    reclining chair invented ("drunken
        lord's chair"), 46

styles of chairs, 43, *44,* 46
T'ang Dynasty, 41, 42
stools in, 42
women in, 42
"Chinese style," 59
Chippendale, Thomas/chairs of, 57–60, *60,*
    62
choir stalls, 26–27, *26*
comb, 63–64
comfortable chairs
    Chinese, 46
    easy chairs, 66
    klismos (light chair), 19–21, *21,* 46
    "overstuffed chairs," 81–82, *82,* 121
    upholstered, 54–55
Cook, Eliza, 82
crest rail, 58, 59
curved-back chairs, *41,* 46, *76,* 109, *110,*
    117, 118
    See also klismos
cushions
    in China, 42
    in Egypt, 14
    in Greece, 20
    in Middle Ages, 30
    in Rome, 22–23

Danko, Peter, 116–19, *117, 118*
Dark Ages, 25
    monasteries in, 25–27
decoration. *See* ornamentation
"De Stijl," 101–3, *102*
dining
    benches, 26, 33, 35
    couches (*triclinium*), 22, *22,* 23
    room, 38
    side chairs, 38
    Wright chairs, *98,* 100

Eames chair, 109, *110*
Eames, Charles and Ray, 108–9, *110*
easy chairs, 66
    experimental, 112
    See also "overstuffed chairs"
Edward I, of Great Britain, chair for,

33–34, *34*
Egypt
    furnishings of ancient, 9, 10–11, *12, 13*
    homes in ancient, 9–10
    IV dynasty, 14
    New Kingdom, 15, 17
    Old Kingdom, 11
    tombs, 9, *12, 13*
    XVIII dynasty, 9–10
Empire style, 75–76
    "chair for an officer," 76
England
    Bath chairs, 77, *79*
    children's chairs introduced, 57
    Chippendale chairs, 57–60, *60*, 62
    Hepplewhite chairs, 60–61, *61, 62*
    Sheraton chairs, 61–62, *62*
    Windsor chairs, 63–64, *64*
    wing chairs, 65–66, *67*

fabric panels for arms/backs/seats, 103–5,
    104
Federal style, 76–77, *76*
folding chairs of Middle Ages, *31*, 32, *32*
folding stools
    Egyptian, 11, *13*
    French, 48
    Greek, 18
    Middle Ages, 32, *32*
    Roman, 24
footrest/footstools, 43, *44*, 66
France
    arrangement of furniture, 51, 53
    "Canopy of State," 51–52
    Empire style, 75–76
    Louis XIV, 47–52, *50*
    Louis XV, *49*, 52–56, *54, 55*
    needlepoint, use of, *50*, 56
    "running chairs," 53–54, *54*
    status and seated furniture in, 48,
        50–52, *52*
    stools, 48, 50
    taborets, 48
    upholstery in, 53–55, *55*, 56
    women and seated furniture, 53

Franklin, Benjamin, *65*, 67–68
"French chairs," 56
furniture making
    beginning of, 3–4
    in America, 66–69, 81
    in China, 43
    cost, 39
    craftsmen, kinds of, 57
    during Dark Ages, by monks, 25–27, *26*
    Egyptian, 10–11, 14, *14*
    English, 57–64, *60, 61, 62*
    French, 53, 54–55, *55*, 56
    Greek, 17–18
    in India, 39–40
    during Middle Ages, 27, 29–30, 33
    See also Chippendale, Thomas; Hepple-
        white, George; Sheraton, Thomas;
        upholstery

Gentleman's and Cabinetmaker's Director
    (Chippendale), 58–59, *60*
George III, 63
Ghana, 97
gilder, 57
gold
    gilding, 15, 17
    leaf, 15
    thrones of, *7*, 91, 96
Golden Stool of the Ashanti, 90–97
"gouty stools," 66
grandfather chairs, 66
Great Britain's coronation chair, 33–34, *34*
Greece, ancient
    houses of, 17
    klismos (light chair), 19–21, *21*
    stools in, 17–19, *18*
    turning first used in, 17–18
    women in, 19, 20–21, *21*
Guggisberg, Sir Gordon, 96

Harington, Sir John, 38
Hepplewhite, George/chairs of, 60–61, *61,
    62*
Hodgson, Sir Frederic, 92–93, *94*
Homer, 19

houses
    American, modern, 121–22
    Arab nomads, 2, *2*
    Egyptian, 9–10
    Greek, 17
    Japanese, 3, *4*, 99
    as machines, 105
    Middle Ages, Europe, 27, *28*, 28–29, 33
    Renaissance, 35
    Roman, 21–22
    Shaker, *72*, 73
    twentieth century, 100–101

India
    caning of chairs, 39–40
    introduction of chairs in, 39
    manufacture of chairs in, 39–40
    platform thrones in, 5, *6*
inlays, for decoration, 15

"Jamaica wood," 59
Japanese people, homes and furnishings
    of
    chairs, 121
    houses, 3
    sitting on floor, 40
    tatami (rice straw mats), 3, *4*
joiner, 57
"Just Moved" (Mosler), *68*

k'angs (sleeping platforms), 40, 42
klismos (light chair), 19–21, *21*, 24, 77

"ladder backs," 70
lamination, 83. *See also* bentwood chairs
Le Corbusier, 105
Louis XIV, King of France, 46, 47–52, *49*,
    50
Louis XV, King of France, 52–56, *54*, *55*

mahogany, 59, *62*
marble, for Greek thrones, 20
men
    and Greek houses, 17
    status and seat furniture, 10, 11, 18–19,

42, *45*, 46, 48, *49*, 50–52
    wigs of, and seated furniture, 60
metal seated furniture
    Barcelona chair, 105–6, *106*
    Breuer (chrome steel tubing), 103–5,
    104, 122
    bronze Roman dining couches, 22
    bronze stools, 24
    iron chairs, *31*
    iron stools, 24
    kitchen chairs, 122
    twentieth century, 106–7
    See also gold
Mickey Mouse chair (Walsh), 113, *115*
Middle Ages
    merchant and craftsman life, 28–29
    peasant life, 27, *28*
    status and chairs, 30, 33
    stools in, 27, *28*, 29
    styles of chairs in, 31–33, *31*, *32*
    typical chair of, 29–30, *30*
misericords, 26, 27
Mondrian, Piet, 101
mortise and tenon construction, 11, 14, *14*
    in China, 43

Napoleon, 75
Nathan, Sir Matthew, 94
needlepoint, *50*, 56, 59
North, Sir Dudley, 39

ornamentation
    animal feet, 15, *16*, 17, 18, *76*
    animal heads, 11, 17
    baroque, 50–51
    carving of African stools/chief's chairs,
    86, 88, *87*, *91*
    of choir stalls, *26*
    of dining couches (Roman), 22–23
    gold leaf/plate, 15, 17, *91*
    inlays, 15
"overstuffed chairs," 81–82, *82*, 121

painter, 57
painting of chairs

Aalto plywood chair, *108*
in Egypt, 15
Rietveld, 102, *102*
Shakers, 74
"Paralytic Woman, A" (Géricault), *78*
perfect chair, search for, 116–21, *117, 118, 120*
Phyfe, Duncan/chairs of, 76–77, *76*
Picasso, Pablo, 97
plastic chairs, 109, *110*
plywood chairs, 107–9, *108*, 116–17, *117*
Prempeh, 92, 96, 97

reclining chair, invented in China ("drunken lord's chair"), 46
Red and Blue Chair, The (Rietveld), *102*
Renaissance
armchairs, *35*, 36–38, *37*
backstools, 35–26
dining rooms introduced in, 38
poor homes in, 35
side chairs, *36*, 38
trade with Far East, 38, 39
upholstered chairs introduced in, 38, *38*
wealthy homes in, 34–35
Rietveld, Gerrit, 101–3, *102*
rocking chair, 66–70, *68, 69, 70, 75*
Rome
atriums, 23
chairs in, 23, *23*, 24
collapse of Roman Empire, 24
dining couches (*triclinium*), 22, *22*, 23
houses in, 21–22, *23*
introduce chair to Western Europe, 24
stools, 23
women in, 23, 24
"running chairs," 53–54, *54*

Saarinen, Eero, 109, 110, *110*
Sabertash, Orlando, 81
Schatmeyer, Gary, *114*
sculpture, chairs as, 111, 113–16, *114, 115, 116*
seat rail, *58*, 59
seats

curved, *13*, 14
fabric, *31*, 103–5, *104*
leather, 11, *13*, 32. *32*, 88
woven, 20, 29
"Sense of Hearing, The," *36*
Shakers, 71–75
chairs of, 70, 74–75, *75*
dwelling, *72*
Sheraton, Thomas/chairs of, 61–62, *62*
side chairs (armless chairs)
baroque (French), 48, 51, 53
bentwood, 83, *84*, 85
Bodyform, *117*
cantilevered chairs, 104–5
Chippendale, 59–60, *60*
Egyptian, *12, 13*, 14, *16*
Federal by Phyfe, *76*
klismos (light chair), 19–21, *21*, 24
origin of name, 38
Renaissance, *36*, 38
Roman, 24
Waveform, *118*
Wright chairs, *98*, 100
Solomon, King of Hebrew people, 7
splat, *58*, 59
State House, Philadelphia, 64, *65*
stiles, *58*, 59
stone as chair material
Burton stools, benches, chairs, 114–16, *116*
for theater seats, 19, *20*
Stone of Scone, *34*
stools
African thrones, 85, *86*, 87–88, 90–91, *91*, 92–94, 96–97
ancient, 5
in China, 42
in Egypt, 10–11, *12, 13*
in France, 48
"gouty," 66
in Greece, 17–19, *18*
in Middle Ages, 27, *28*, 29, 32, *32*
prehistoric, 3
in Renaissance, 35
in Rome, 23–24

stretcher, *58*, 58–59
Sweerts, Michael, *35*

taborets, 48
tatami (rice straw mats), 3, *4*
theater seats, 19, *20*, 27
Thonet, Michael, 83, *84*, 85
Thoreau, Henry David, v
throne(s)
    of Africa, 85
    of Buddha, 5, *6*
    in Denmark, *52*
    Great Britain's coronation chair, 33–34,
        34
    for Greek gods, 19
    at Greek theater, 19, *20*
    of King Solomon, 7
    -like chairs, 33
    platform, 5
    of Tutankhamen, *16*, 17
triclinium (couch), 22, *22*, 23
turning (woodworking technique), 17–18
Tutankhamen, tomb of, 9, *13*, *16*, 17
Tutu, Osei, 90–91

upholstered chairs
    of foam rubber, 109
    French, 53–55, *55*, 56
    "French chairs," 56
    needlepoint, use of, *50*, 56, 59
    "overstuffed chairs," 81–82, *82*
    Renaissance, *37*, 38
    Saarinen's use of, 109, *111*
    springs, use of, 53–54, 78, 81
    unknown to Egyptians, 14
    unknown during Middle Ages, 30
upholsterer, 57

van der Rohe, Mies, 103–6, *106*
Versailles, 46, 47–50

Walden (Thoreau), v
Walsh, Catherine, *115*
Watervliet, New York, 72
Waveform chair (Danko), *118*, 118–19

wheelchair, 77, *78*, *79*, *80*
wicker chairs in ancient Rome, 24
    See also caning of chairs
Windsor chairs, 63–64, *64*, *65*
    bow of, 63
    comb of, 63–64
wing chairs, 65–66, *67*
"womb chair," *110*
women
    in China, and stools, 42
    corsets of, and seated furniture, 60, 100
    and Empire style, 75
    and farthingale (hoopskirt), 36, *37*
    in France, and armchairs, 53
    in Greece, 17, 19
    and *klismos*, 19–21, *21*
wood
    benches, 26, 33
    bentwood, 83, *84*, 85
    chairs, 10–11, *13*, 19–21, *21*, *23*, 24, *31*,
        42, *44*, 46, 59, *62*, 63–64, *64*, *65*, 69,
        69, 70, 74, *75*, *76*, 88, *89*
    choir stalls, *26*
    disadvantages of, 40
    Great Britain's coronation chair,
        33–34, *34*
    kinds of used in chair-making, 11, 59,
        62, 69, 74, 83
    Middle Ages, typical chair of, 29–30,
        30
    mortise and tenon construction, 11, 14,
        14
    plywood, 107–9, *108*, 116–17, *117*
    stools, 10, *12*, *13*, 17–19, *18*, 24, *32*, 42,
        86, 87, 90, *91*, *98*, *102*
    turning, 17–18
Wright, Frank Lloyd, 97, *98*, 99–100